lonely planet

POCKET

ATHENS

TOP EXPERIENCES • LOCAL LIFE

ZORA O'NEILL

Contents

Plan Your Trip

Temple of Olympian Zeus (p116)
PEL_1971/GETTY IMAGES ©

COVID-19

We have re-checked every business in this book before publication to ensure that it is still open after the COVID-19 outbreak. However, the economic and social impacts of COVID-19 will continue to be felt long after the outbreak has been contained, and many businesses, services and events referenced in this guide may experience ongoing restrictions. Some may be temporarily closed, have changed their opening hours and services, or require bookings; some unfortunately could have closed permanently. We suggest you check with venues before visiting for the latest information.

Top Experiences

Explore Ancient Greece at the Acropolis

An icon of Western civilisation. **p34**

Examine Treasures at the Acropolis Museum
The Parthenon at eye level. **p40**

Step into the Past at the Ancient Agora
The heart of classical Athens. **p54**

Immerse Yourself at the Benaki Museum of Greek Culture
Private mansion turned public treasure. **p100**

Admire Antiquities at the National Archaeological Museum
Greece's finest classical treasures. **p128**

Wander the Ruins at Kerameikos
A cemetery reveals ancient life. **p158**

Stroll up Filopappou Hill
Ancient history and green space. **p148**

Marvel at the Temple of Olympian Zeus

Emperor Hadrian's biggest building project. **p116**

Dining Out

Eating, drinking and talking is the main entertainment for Athenians. The current restaurant scene is vibrant, and some of the best cooking is found in just-slightly-modernised tavernas that showcase fresh produce and regional ingredients. Add in a culture of convivial alfresco dining, and no wonder meals tend to last for hours.

Restaurant Types

Tavernas are neighbourhood anchors. A *psarotaverna* focuses on seafood; a *hasapotaverna* or *psistaria* does meat. Also casual, a *mayirio* specialises in home-style stews and baked dishes *(mayirefta)*. More formal is the *estiatorio*, with cloth on the tables.

Casual *ouzeries* and *mezedhopoleia* both serve small plates with drinks. Souvlaki (aka *kalamaki*) is Athens' favourite fast food; restaurants that do these grilled meat skewers usually also do *gyros* (slivers of meat cooked on a vertical rotisserie).

What Looks Good

In summer, an empty room doesn't necessarily mean bad – it could just be that everyone is on the roof terrace or in the courtyard.

At mom-and-pop places, it's normal to go into the kitchen to see the day's dishes.

For other tips on ordering, see Menu Advice (p166).

Best Traditional Greek

Telis Pork chops, grilled by a master. (p68)

Diporto Agoras Legendary cheap lunch spot near the central market. (p75)

I Kriti Super-rustic Cretan specialities. (p139)

Palia Athina Checked tablecloths: check. Perfect calamari: check. (p87)

Kalderimi A taste of the village downtown. (p86)

Atlantikos The freshest seafood, simply prepared. (p68)

Best Mezedhes

Ivis Watch the Psyrri scene from a little table at this sweet corner bar-cafe. (p67)

LAMBROS KAZANN/SHUTTERSTOCK ©

Glykys Complement ouzo with meatballs, spicy sausages and other classics at this Plaka courtyard spot. (p87)

Ama Laxei stis Nefelis At this converted school you'll learn about the vast variety of seasonal Greek food. (p140)

Best Modern Greek

Mavro Provato The best of Athens' modern tavernas. (p122)

Karamanlidika tou Fani The corner butcher, reimagined as a restaurant. (p65)

Seychelles How can one restaurant be so good, so cool and so cheap? (p165)

Spondi A beautiful garden setting and Michelin-lauded food. (p122)

Best Snacks & Sweets

Elvis Excellent-quality meat goes into the skewers at this rockin' souvlaki joint. (p165)

Feyrouz Fresh, healthy and spicy – a budget diner's best friend. (p59)

Bougatsadiko I Thessaloniki Spinach, cheese and pies, made in the most traditional way. (p65)

Cremino Sumptuous gelato and sorbet. (p87)

Kostas Eat your souvlaki standing. (p65)

Standard Practices

• Athenians start eating dinner around 9pm.

• For trendy restaurants, book ahead on weekends (try www.e-table.gr), or go early.

• Plates are typically not cleared until you ask for the bill (and you must ask for it).

Bar Open

In Athens the line between cafe and bar is blurry. Most places segue from coffee to drinks, and maybe music and a DJ, at night. There is almost always food – although places that serve only drinks are more common in the economic crisis (in which case, you can bring your own snacks). The smoking ban is often ignored.

Neighbourhoods

Gazi and Kolonaki tend toward slicker, spendier clubs. For cheaper drinks and live music, head for Keramikos or Exarhia. Psyrri and north of Syntagma are the best central areas for interesting bars.

Greek Music

Traditional music pops up all over. Bars and tavernas – especially in Plaka, Psyrri and Exarhia – host bands evenings and Sunday afternoons. More

formal clubs operate September to May, start around 11.30pm and do not have a cover charge (though drinks are pricier than in bars).

Summer Clubs

In summer, Athenians decamp to mega-clubs along the seafront in Glyfada, along the tram line. If you book for dinner you don't pay cover; otherwise admission ranges from €10 to €20 and includes one drink. Glam up to get in.

Best Neighbourhood Bars

Six d.o.g.s. One of the best in Psyrri: indoor-outdoor, rooms upon rooms. (p69)

Ippo In the Syntagma bar zone, but with a loyal crew of regulars. (p90)

Chelsea Hotel Pangrati-style chill, packed day and night. (p124)

Galaxy Bar A gorgeous old vintage space, hidden in a Syntagma arcade. (p79)

Nabokov Low-key literati spot on the edge of Exarhia. (p141)

Alphaville The Keramikos (night) lifestyle in a nutshell. (p161)

ENTRECHAT/GETTY IMAGES ©

Best Speciality Bars

Baba Au Rum Takes umbrella drinks seriously. (p89)

Clumsies Repeatedly cited for world's best bartenders. (p90)

Heteroclito Lovely unpretentious wine bar. (p90)

Barley Cargo The Greek beer experts. (p90)

Best Cafes

Taf Coffee House roasted, perfectly brewed. (p141)

Veneti A more recent name on a classic two-storey grand cafe in Omonia. (p141)

Little Tree Book Cafe Coffee, wine and snacks with local bookworms. (p47)

Spiti Mas Take your morning coffee in a mock-up apartment. (p70)

Best Photo Ops

Couleur Locale The Acropolis looks close enough to touch at this rooftop bar. (p70)

Little Kook The view in this case is not the Acropolis, but the wild decor. (p70)

Noel Everyone looks photogenic in this beautifully lit bar. (p70)

Yiasemi Look at you, sipping a drink on the most scenic steps in Plaka! (p89)

Nightlife Tips

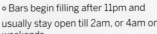

○ Bars begin filling after 11pm and usually stay open till 2am, or 4am on weekends.

○ Public transport stops or slows after midnight, but cabs are very cheap.

○ For more, see Party Smart (p91).

Treasure Hunt

Central Athens is the city's original commercial district, and one big shopping hub, with an eclectic mix of stores. The area is still organised roughly by category – lace and buttons on one block, light bulbs on the next. The main (if generic) shopping street is pedestrianised Ermou, running from Syntagma to Monastiraki.

Style Hunting

As with many creative endeavours in Athens, fashion and design are flourishing. For the shopper who wants what no one else has yet, Alternative Athens (p20) runs tours of designers' workshops.

Sales and Pricing

August to September and January to February are the big months for sales, especially on clothes. Bargaining is acceptable at flea markets, and perhaps gently at dustier antiques dealers, but in general prices are fixed.

Best Creative Souvenirs

Korres Stock up on this Greek beauty brand. (p93)

Forget Me Not The original dealer in smart souvenirs and other cool design items, all with a Hellenic twist. (p93)

Flâneur Love feta? Show your loyalty with a cute pin or patch. (p93)

TAF This gallery-cafe also has a very cool design shop. (p64)

138 Pireos St The gift shop at this contemporary art museum is top-notch. (p163)

Best Arts & Crafts

Amorgos Handmade puppets and toys. (p93)

Benaki Museum of Greek Culture Excellent handicrafts in the gift shop. (p100)

Zoumboulakis Gallery Prints of work by some of Greece's finest artists. (p113)

Hrisanthos Spread the worry-bead habit with a set from this old shop. (p59)

Monastiraki Flea Market Dusty treasures are waiting to be discovered. (pictured; p59)

El.Marneri Galerie Local modern art and super jewellery. (p49)

MATTEO COLOMBO/GETTY IMAGES ©

Best Accessories

Lemisios Classic shoe shop that can customise its designs. (p112)

Katerina Ioannidis Delicate jewellery with a folkloric touch. (p112)

Melissinos Art The (son of the) 'poet sandal maker' is an Athens legend. (p73)

Zacharias Lovely leather goods screen-printed with ancient patterns. (p144)

Best Food

Varvakios Agora Maybe you don't need a whole lamb, but you do need to see the city's central market. (p75)

Exarhia Weekly Market Athens' neighbourhood veg markets are a treat; this

is a great one. (Map p136; ⊙6am-2pm Sat; 🚇026 , MOmonia)

Pantopoleion Much more than the usual grocery store, this shop stocks excellent regional items. (p75)

Mastiha Shop All kinds of products featuring this only-on-Chios miracle resin. (p112)

Best Music

Yiannis Samouelin Best bouzoukis in town. (p72)

Xylouris Traditional Cretan music, instruments and general knowledge. (p94)

Plan 59 Especially good selection of Greek vinyl. (p144)

Typical Shop Hours

○ Normal closing (5pm or so): Monday, Wednesday, Saturday.

○ Late (8pm, sometimes with an afternoon break): Tuesday, Thursday, Friday.

○ Exception: Plaka tourist shops, always open late.

Show Time

The Athens arts and music scene depends largely on the season: many big halls and theatres close or scale back programming in the summer, when open-air spaces take over. Bonus: Greeks consider every musical event an opportunity for a singalong, which can make the most formal concert venues feel chummy (even if you don't know the words).

Athens & Epidaurus Festival

June to August is time for this world-class festival (p20) of local and international music, dance and drama at the ancient Odeon of Herodes Atticus at the Acropolis. It's absolutely worth planning around.

Open-Air Cinema

One of the delights of Athens is watching the latest Hollywood or art-house flick in the warm summer air. The settings are old-fashioned gardens and rooftops, with modern sound and projection. Cinemas start up in early May and usually close in September. For movie times, see **Athinorama** (www.athinorama.gr), which has a filter for outdoor theatres; use a browser translator, as it's Greek only.

Listings & Tickets

Check the **Kathimerini English Edition** (www.ekathimerini.com), also a print supplement to the *International New York Times* and **This Is Athens** (www.thisisathens.gr). Greek site **ελculture** (www.elculture.gr) is more comprehensive. **Viva** (www.viva.gr) is a major ticket vendor.

Best Multiuse Spaces

Gazarte Multiple venues in this big building in Gazi. (p167)

TAF A cluster of 19th-century buildings with a great courtyard cafe. (p64)

Treno sto Rouf A cool bar and cabaret, plus occasional creative performance, in old rail cars. (p168)

Bios Industrial chic with a cinema, a gallery, a bar and more. (p169)

MILAN GONDA/SHUTTERSTOCK ©

Best Big Venues

National Theatre English-language surtitles for many performances. (p143)

Technopolis Open-air music hall in the converted gasworks. (pictured; p169)

Stavros Niarchos Foundation Cultural Center Tons of programming year-round here, including the Greek National Opera. (p171)

Best Live Music

Afrikana Jazz and world music in a small converted house. (p169)

Kavouras *Rembetika* club above a souvlaki joint in Exarhia. (p143)

Half Note Jazz Club The city's premier jazz venue. (p124)

Feidiou 2 Music Cafe Informal and intimate. (p143)

Akordeon Friendly hosts serve delicious local eats and get the whole taverna dancing with their songs. (p67)

Best Open-Air Cinemas

Cine Paris Claims to be the oldest open-air cinema, in a prime Plaka location. (p91)

Thission The Acropolis view competes for attention. (p154)

Riviera Eclectic and artsy programming at this Exarhia favourite. (p143)

Worth a Trip

The city's state-of-the-art concert hall, **Megaron Mousikis** (Athens Concert Hall; www.megaron.gr), presents a rich winter program of operas and concerts. In summer it has shows in the back garden. The Music Library of Greece is also located here, with some 10,000 sound recordings.

Museums & History

Without a doubt, Athens' top draw is its ancient ruins and the blockbuster museums dedicated to this same period. But a city this old has many more layers of history, and many other critical artistic moments – and some excellent museums, churches and other patches of hallowed ground.

Best Art Museums

138 Pireos St Rotating exhibits of primarily modern and contemporary art in a cool converted industrial space. (p163)

National Museum of Contemporary Art In a remodelled brewery, see contemporary Greek and international art stars. (p43)

Museum of Cycladic Art Connecting ancient art with modern, featuring the minimalist sculptures that inspired Picasso and Modigliani. (p106)

Museum of Islamic Art Jaw-droppingly beautiful examples of pottery, jewellery, weaving and more from the Middle East and Asia. (pictured; p163)

Byzantine & Christian Museum Is it art? Is it culture? It's simply beautiful. (p106)

Best Historical Sites

Koraï 4 A legacy of Nazi occupation. (p79)

Theatre of Dionysos The birthplace of theatre, on the Acropolis' southern slopes. (p39)

Hill of the Pnyx Athens' ancient democratic assembly met and debated here. (p151)

National Historical Museum In the old Parliament building, where Prime Minister Theodoros Deligiannis was assassinated on the front steps in 1905. (p84)

Aristotle's Lyceum Where the famed philosopher led his students on thoughtful walks. (p107)

Best Speciality Museums

Jewish Museum Explore the deep roots of Greek Jews. (p82)

MILAN GONDA/SHUTTERSTOCK ©

Numismatic Museum Go for the coins, stay for the mansion. Or vice versa. (p106)

Dora Stratou Dance Theatre The folklorist who founded this dance troupe considered it a 'living museum' of Greek tradition. (p155)

Museum of Greek Folk Art at 22 Panos If you like the agriculture section at the Benaki Museum, you'll love this. (p85)

Best Byzantine Churches

Church of Agios Dimitrios Loumbardiaris Site of an alleged miracle in 1648, when a lightning strike is said to have saved the congregation from Turkish attack. (p149)

Church of Agios Eleftherios Look for the nude pagan relief on the north outside wall. (p63)

Church of Sotira Lykodimou Built in the 11th century, with 19th-century icons. (p84)

Top Tips

○ Outside of peak summer, most sites and museums close by early afternoon –and small museums may have limited hours year-round. Confirm hours before setting out.

○ Churches have no set opening times; just duck in whenever you see one open.

○ Eligible for reduced entrance? See Discount Cards (p178).

Active Athens

LAMBROS KAZAN/SHUTTERSTOCK ©

With its winding streets, Athens rewards random wandering and unstructured exploration. But some excellent tour guides and other activities can help you dig deeper, and some special events may shape your itinerary too. Activities that don't require pre-planning are listed in the relevant chapters.

Best Tours

This Is My Athens (http://myathens.thisisathens.org) City-run program pairs you with a volunteer local. Book 72 hours ahead.

Alternative Athens (☎6951518589; www.alternativeathens.com; Karaïskaki 28; Ⓜ Monastiraki, Thissio) As the name implies, tours with less-typical slants.

Roll in Athens (☎6974231611; www.rollinathens.tours; Voreou 10; half-day tours €30; Ⓜ Monastiraki, Omonia) Take a bike tour around the centre – or better still, down to the seaside.

Solebike (☎210 921 5620; www.solebike.eu; Lembesi 11, Makrygianni; 3hr from €45; ☉9am-5pm Mon-Sat Apr-Nov, 10am-4pm Mon-Sat Sep-Mar; Ⓜ Akropoli) See the sights on an electric bike.

Best Arts Events

Athens & Epidaurus Festival (Hellenic Festival; ☎210 928 2900; www.greekfestival.gr; ☉Jun-Aug) Since 1955, Athens' premier arts event, set in an ancient theatre.

Athens Biennale (☎210 523 2222; www.athensbiennale.org; ☉Oct-Dec) Cultural event which hosts exhibitions, performances and workshops - check the webite to see next scheduled edition.

Athens Technopolis Jazz Festival (www.technopolisjazzfestival.com; ☉late May-early Jun) In Gazi and the excellent Onassis Cultural Centre.

August Moon Festival On the night of the full moon, ancient sites host music and art.

Best Food Activities

Athens Walking Tours (☎210 884 7269; www.athenswalkingtours.gr; Heyden 2, Viktoria; Ⓜ Viktoria) Its cooking class shows how to roll your own filo for *spanakopita* (spinach pie).

Athens Street Food Festival (☎210 963 6489; www.athensstreetfoodfestival.gr; ☉May) Instantly popular when it started in 2016.

Cycle Greece (☎210 921 8160; www.cyclegreece.com) Runs a day bike tour of Athens-area wineries.

Under the Radar Athens

Athens hasn't endured for over 3500 years by standing still. The city is constantly evolving, and there's always something new bubbling up for the curious visitor to discover beyond the heavily trafficked tourist hot spots. To immerse yourself in a more local version of Athens head to the following neighbourhoods.

EQROY/SHUTTERSTOCK © ARTIST: STMTS

Kypseli

Kypseli, a 15-minute walk north of Exarhia, was once one of the most desirable residential areas of Athens, on a par with Kolonaki. It's not so ritzy today, even though if you keep an eye out there's still the odd pretty neoclassical mansion or art deco block to be found among the dense streets of identikit five-storey Athens apartment blocks.

The neighbourhood's social centre is the Fokionos Negri pedestrian strip of park, lined with cafes. **Kypseli Municipal Market** (https://agorakypselis.gr; Fokionos Negri 42, Kypseli; ⊙9am-9pm Mon-Fri, 10am-7pm Sat) This 1935 modernist building, houses a range of social projects including the non-profit business Wise Greece, which sells some 2500 good-quality food products from across the country.

Metaxourgio

Epic scale street art abounds in Metaxourgio. To discover some of the best works join one of **Alternative Athens** (p20) excellent themed walking tours of this area and neighbouring Gazi. **The Breeder** (📞210 331 7527; http://thebreedersystem. com; Iasonos 45, Metaxourgio; ⊙noon-8pm Tue-Fri, to 6pm Sat; Ⓜ Metaxourgio) is a hip concrete warehouse-style art gallery; every year they reinvent their exterior design as an art project.

Pangrati

Pangrati's Plateia Varnava is a great place to experience a typical Athenian neighbourhood, with families dining in the tavernas and kids playing in the square. Buy a snack from the bakery **Kallimarmaro** (p122) and a soda from the periptero (kiosk) and sit and enjoy the scene.

LGBTIQ+

Greece's reputation as a millennia-old gay-friendly culture sometimes clashes with contemporary Orthodox mores: gay marriage is not yet legal, for example. But Athens' LGBTIQ+ scene is lively and increasingly becoming an international draw. Athens Pride (pictured), held in June, has been an annual event since 2005.

KOSTAS KOUTSAFTIKIS/SHUTTERSTOCK ©

Neighbourhoods

For nightlife, Gazi is Athens' main LGBTIQ+ hub, with both a few big mega-clubs and, more on the fringes of the area, some good small bars. Gay-friendly cafes can also be found around Plateia Agia Irini and in Metaxourgio and Exarhia. Alternative Athens (p20) runs a bar crawl tour around some of the neighbourhoods.

Best by Night

BeQueer The new generation of LGBTIQ+ nightlife. (p167)

S-Cape Long-established mega-club in Gazi. (p168)

Noiz Club Also in Gazi, for women. (p161)

Big The main outpost of Athens' lively bear scene. (p168)

Koukles Old-school drag in Koukaki. (p49)

Best by Day

Loukoumi There's always something happening at this multiuse arts space. (p72)

Myrovolos A popular lesbian spot. Greek meals available. (p161)

Beaver Collective Women run this cafe by the Benaki Pireos annexe. (p168)

Rooster Cafe and cocktails in the centre of Monastiraki's booming scene, on Plateia Agia Irini. (p71)

Online info

For more recommendations and events:

Athens Pride (www.athenspride.eu)

Athens Info Guide (www.athensinfoguide.com)

Athens Real (www.athens-real.com)

For Kids

Athens is short on playgrounds, but between ice cream and street musicians and stray cats, there's plenty to keep kids amused. It helps too that children are welcome everywhere, and at casual restaurants they're often encouraged to run off and play together while the adults eat.

NADYAEUGENE/SHUTTERSTOCK ©

Movie Magic

Outdoor cinema makes even a Hollywood blockbuster special. Only films for the youngest kids are dubbed; everything else gets Greek subtitles.

Shadow Puppets

Younger children may enjoy Greece's shadow-puppet tradition. Shows are in Greek, but it's really all about the slapstick comedy and music.

Best Spectacles

Theatro Skion Tasou Konsta Shadow-puppet theatre in the kid-friendly Flisvos Park; moves to Plaka in winter. (p171)

Melina Merkouri Cultural Centre Shadow-puppet shows on Sundays year-round. (p152)

Cine Paris Lovely open-air movies, right in the centre. (p91)

Little Kook Fairy tales and children's books come to life at this fantastically decorated cafe. (p70)

Best Parks & Gardens

National Gardens A playground, duck pond and bare-bones zoo. (p82)

Stavros Niarchos Park Grand modern park south of the centre; rent a bike to roam. (p171)

Lykavittos Hill Admire the whole city from the peak. Bonus: novelty funicular ride. (p99)

Latraac Skate park meets cafe. (p164)

Best Museums & Tours

Museum of Greek Children's Art Dedicated space for kids to learn about Ancient Greece. (www.childrensartmuseum.gr; €3; ⊙10am-2pm Tue-Sat, 11am-2pm Sun; Ⓜ Syntagma)

War Museum Good for teens; they can climb in the cockpit of a WWII plane. (p106)

Athens Happy Train All aboard this mini tour bus/train. (p86)

Four Perfect Days

Day 1

RICARDO DE MATTOS/GETTY IMAGES ©

Get oriented by walking a circle around the centre, starting early at the glorious **Acropolis** (pictured; p34). Wind down to the **Roman Agora** (p62) and the **Ancient Agora** (p54). Lunch at souvlaki legend **Thanasis** (p66), then stroll and shop along Plaka's **Adrianou Street** to close the loop.

From here, head to the **Acropolis Museum** (p40) and its masterpieces. Close to sundown, join the crowds strolling on Dionysiou Areopagitou, and walk up **Filopappou Hill** (p148). Dine with an Acropolis view at **Strofi** (p44).

Catch an outdoor movie at **Thission** (p154) or **Cine Paris** (p91) in Plaka. In cooler weather have a cosy drink at **Brettos** (p91).

Day 2

HERACLES KRITIKOS/SHUTTERSTOCK ©

At the **Tomb of the Unknown Soldier** (p82) watch the *evzones* (guards) strut their pom-pom-toed stuff. Then walk to the **Benaki Museum of Greek Culture** (p100). Lunch at the museum.

Stroll south through the gardens of the **Byzantine & Christian Museum** (p106) to the old **Panathenaic Stadium** (p120), then pass by the **Temple of Olympian Zeus** (p116) and **Hadrian's Arch** (p51).

Have dinner in Pangrati at **Mavro Provato** (p122), or head for Monastiraki (pictured), conveniently near bars like **Six d.o.g.s.** (p69) and **Noel** (p70). If you need snacks, you'll find options on Athinaidos.

Day 3

SAIKO3P/SHUTTERSTOCK ©

First things first: the treasures of the **National Archaeological Museum** (p128). Walk or bus to the **Athens Central Market** (p75). Have lunch at **Diporto Agoras** (p75) or **Karamanlidika tou Fani** (p65).

Head to Kolonaki for window-shopping or more museums: **Museum of Cycladic Art** (p106) and the **Byzantine & Christian Museum** (p106) are both excellent. At sunset, take the funicular up **Lykavittos Hill** (pictured; p99), then eat dinner back downhill at **Filippou** (p103) or **Oikeio** (p108)

End with cocktails at one of the excellent Syntagma-area bars, such as **Galaxy Bar** (p79). If you prefer casual beers instead, head to Exarhia.

Day 4

WESTEND61/GETTY IMAGES ©

Immerse yourself in the archaeological site of **Kerameikos** (pictured; p158), then visit the nearby **Museum of Islamic Art** (p163). Or if you're footsore from sightseeing, revive with a bath at **Hammam** (p164), then have lunch at **Ivis** (p67) or **Atlantikos** (p68)

Get a shot of contemporary art at **138 Pireos St** (p163). The cafe here is nice for coffee – or cross the road to **Upopa Epops** (p154). For dinner head up to Thisio's **Steki tou Ilia** (p152), or to **Seychelles** (p165) in Metaxourgio.

Explore music venues in Gazi: a DJ at **Gazarte** (p167) or **Bios** (p169), or a jazz band at **Afrikana** (p169). And there's almost always a traditional Greek group playing at **Steki Pinoklis** (p169).

Need to Know

For detailed information, see Survival Guide p173

Population
3.1 million

Currency
Euro (€)

Language
Greek

Visas
Generally not required
for stays of up to 90
days.

Money
Major banks have
branches around
Syntagma. ATMs are
only in commercial
districts.

Time
Eastern European Time
(GMT/UTC plus two
hours)

Phones
EU phones have free
roaming. Or buy an
inexpensive GSM SIM
card at phone shops;
bring your passport.

Tipping
If service charge added
on restaurant bill,
round to nearest euro.
If not, tip 10% to 20%.

Daily Budget

Budget: Less than €130
Dorm bed: €25
Pension double: from €75
Souvlaki or *pitta* (pie): €2.50
Ouzo with snack: €3
90-minute transit ticket: €1.40

Midrange: €130–250
Double in midrange hotel: €90–180
Traditional taverna meal: €12–15
Museum and site entry fees: €5–20
Taxi across town: €5

Top End: More than €250
Double room in top hotel: from €180
Trendy taverna meal: from €20
Cocktail: €10
Acropolis tour guide: €75

Advance Planning

Three months before Reserve your hotel
early, as the best places fill quickly.

One month before Check the cultural
calendar and book tickets for a performance
at the Odeon of Herodes Atticus, the National
Theatre or Megaron Mousikis. Reserve a table
at top restaurants.

One week before Check online for strike
information (http://livingingreece.gr/strikes);
book tours.

Arriving in Athens

✈ Eleftherios Venizelos International Airport

In Spata, 27km east of Athens.

Metro €10, 50 minutes to Monastiraki, every 30 minutes, 6.30am to 11.30pm

Bus €6, one hour to 1½ hours to Syntagma, every 20 to 30 minutes, 24 hours

Taxi Flat fare to the centre day/night €38/54, 30 to 45 minutes

⚓ Port of Piraeus

Greece's main port, southwest of Athens.

Metro €1.40, 30 minutes to Thissio, frequently 6.30am to 11.30pm

Bus €4, from cruise port to Syntagma in 30 minutes, and on to major sights, May to October only

Taxi €20 to €25 on the meter, 20 minutes

Getting Around

Central Athens is best explored on foot.

🚇 Metro

Three lines, wheelchair-accessible. Runs frequently 5.30am to 12.30am, till 2.30am Friday and Saturday in the centre.

🚌 Bus

Thorough, but no printed map; use Google Maps directions. Most useful: trolleybuses 2, 5, 11, and 15.

🚋 Tram

Scenic but slow way to the coast from Syntagma, 5.30am to 1am, till 2.30am Friday and Saturday.

🚕 Taxi

Inexpensive. Hail on street or use apps **Beat** (www.thebeat.co/gr) or **Taxiplon** (www.taxiplon.gr). Surcharges for luggage; night/holiday rate is 60% higher.

Athens Neighbourhoods

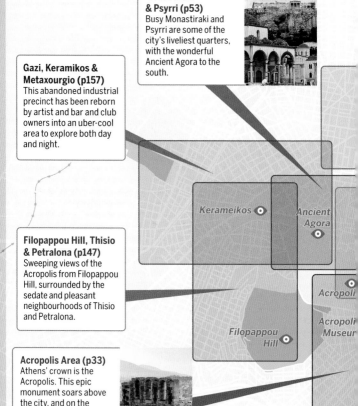

Monastiraki & Psyrri (p53)
Busy Monastiraki and Psyrri are some of the city's liveliest quarters, with the wonderful Ancient Agora to the south.

Gazi, Keramikos & Metaxourgio (p157)
This abandoned industrial precinct has been reborn by artist and bar and club owners into an uber-cool area to explore both day and night.

Filopappou Hill, Thisio & Petralona (p147)
Sweeping views of the Acropolis from Filopappou Hill, surrounded by the sedate and pleasant neighbourhoods of Thisio and Petralona.

Acropolis Area (p33)
Athens' crown is the Acropolis. This epic monument soars above the city, and on the hill's southern slopes, a fabulous modern museum holds its treasures.

Kerameikos

Ancient Agora

Acropoli

Acropoli Museur

Filopappou Hill

Omonia & Exarhia (p127)

Omonia is home to the fabulous National Archaeological Museum, while nearby Exarhia has an interesting mix of students, activists, artists and immigrants.

◉ National Archaeological Museum

Kolonaki (p99)

Kolonaki is an adjective as much as a district: chic, stylish, elite. For visitors, it's also the location of several excellent museums and is a delightfully green area.

Syntagma & Plaka (p77)

Narrow streets, neoclassical mansions, Byzantine churches and tavernas, Plaka is ground zero for Athens tourism, while Syntagma is the heart of modern Athens.

◉ Benaki Museum of Greek Culture

◉ Temple of Olympian Zeus

Mets & Pangrati (p115)

The attractive districts of Mets and Pangrati surround the Panathenaic Stadium, with unpretentious neighbourhoods and low-key-cool places to eat

Explore
Athens

View of the Acropolis (p34) over Monastiraki (p53) MILAN GONDA/SHUTTERSTOCK ©

Explore ⊚

Acropolis Area

Athens' crown is the Acropolis, and its jewel is the Parthenon. This epic monument soars above the city, and on the hill's southern slopes a fabulous modern museum holds its treasures. A pedestrian promenade between the two is a tourist throughway, and a favourite local spot for a sundown stroll. Off this strip, further south, the quiet neighbourhoods of Makrygianni and Koukaki deliver a slice of residential Athens life.

Visitors to Athens naturally make a beeline to the Acropolis (p34); allow at least an hour and a half, and try to go at opening time, to beat big tour groups. (Alternatively, go at least 90 minutes before closing, and head straight for the Parthenon, which the staff start clearing first, then work your way down the south slope.) Either way, reserve midday for the air-conditioned confines of the Acropolis Museum (p40); you can eat lunch here too. After a stroll on the pedestrian road, have dinner with an Acropolis view, or head south for more local options. Shoppers may want to come this way earlier in the day, for the little strip of creative boutiques on Veïkou.

Getting There & Around

Ⓜ Akropoli (red line) sits near the Acropolis Museum and the Acropolis east entrance, just off the major boulevard Leoforos Syngrou.

Ⓜ Monastiraki (blue line) or Thissio (green line) stops are farther away, a scenic walk to the Acropolis' western entrance.

Neighbourhood Map on p42

Caryatids, Acropolis (p38) PAVLEMARJANOVIC/SHUTTERSTOCK IMAGES ©

Top Experience 📷

Explore Ancient Greece at the Acropolis

The Acropolis is the most important ancient site in the Western world. Crowned by the Parthenon, it's visible from almost everywhere in Athens. Its marble gleams white in the midday sun and takes on a honey hue as the sun sinks, then glows above the city by night. A glimpse of this magnificent sight cannot fail to exalt your spirit.

◉ MAP P42, B1

http://odysseus.culture.gr

adult/concession/child €20/10/free

🕑8am-8pm May-Sep, reduced hours in winter, last entry 30min before closing

Ⓜ Akropoli

Parthenon

The Parthenon (pictured) is the monument that more than any other epitomises the glory of Ancient Greece. It is dedicated to Athena Parthenos, the goddess embodying the power and prestige of the city. The largest Doric temple ever completed in Greece, and the only one built completely of Pentelic marble (apart from the wood in its roof), it was designed by Iktinos and Kallicrates to be the pre-eminent monument of the Acropolis and was completed in time for the Great Panathenaic Festival of 438 BCE.

Columns

The Parthenon's fluted Doric columns achieve perfect form. The eight columns at either end and 17 on each side were ingeniously curved to create an optical illusion: the foundations (like all the 'horizontal' surfaces of the temple) are slightly concave and the columns are slightly convex making both appear straight. Supervised by Pheidias, the sculptors Agoracritos and Alcamenes worked on the architectural sculptures of the Parthenon, including the pediments, frieze and metopes, which were brightly coloured and gilded.

Pediments

The temple's pediments (the triangular elements topping the east and west facades) were filled with elaborately carved three-dimensional sculptures. The west side depicted Athena and Poseidon in their contest for the city's patronage, the east Athena's birth from Zeus' head. See their remnants and the rest of the Acropolis' sculptures and artefacts in the Acropolis Museum.

Metopes & Frieze

The Parthenon's metopes, designed by Pheidias, are square carved panels set between channelled triglyphs. The metopes on the eastern side depicted the Olympian gods fighting the giants, and on the western side they showed Theseus leading the Athenian youths into battle against

★ **Top Tips**

o Visit first thing in the morning or late in the day.

o The main entrance is from Dionysiou Areopagitou near the Odeon of Herodes Atticus. The east entrance, near the Akropoli metro, can be less crowded.

o Large bags must be checked, at the main (west) entrance.

o Wheelchairs access the site via a cage lift; call ahead to arrange (☎ 210 321 4172).

o Buy the Acropolis combo ticket at a smaller tourist site, to avoid the ticket-booth line at the Acropolis.

o Check www.culture. gr for free-admission holidays and changing opening hours.

✗ **Take a Break**

Swing in to Dionysos (p46) for coffee and excellent views of the monument.

Or book ahead for a late-afternoon lunch at Mani Mani (p44).

the Amazons. The southern metopes illustrated the contest of the Lapiths and centaurs at a marriage feast, while the northern ones depicted the sacking of Troy. The internal cella was topped by the Ionic frieze, a continuous sculptured band depicting the Panathenaic Procession.

Statue of Athena Polias

The statue for which the temple was built – the Athena Polias (Athena of the City) – was considered one of the wonders of the ancient world. It was taken to Constantinople in CE 426, where it disappeared. Designed by Pheidias and completed in 432 BCE, it stood almost 12m high on its pedestal and was plated in gold. Athena's face, hands and feet were made of ivory, and the eyes fashioned from jewels.

Temple of Poseidon

Though he didn't win patronage of the city, Poseidon was worshipped on the northern side of the Erechtheion. The porch still bears the mark of his trident-strike. Imagine the finely decorated coffered porch painted in rich colours, as it was before.

Erechtheion

The Erechtheion, completed around 406 BCE, was a sanctuary built on the most sacred part of the Acropolis: the spot where Poseidon struck the ground with his trident, and where Athena produced the olive tree. Named after Erechtheus, a mythical king of Athens, the temple housed the cults of Athena, Poseidon and Erechtheus. This supreme example of Ionic architecture was ingeniously built on several

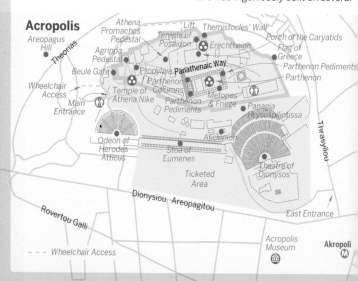

The Acropolis Through History

Contest for Athens

The founding of Athens is enshrined in myth. Phoenician king Kekrops, the story goes, founded a city on a huge rock near the sea. The gods of Olympus proclaimed that it should be named for the deity who could provide the most valuable legacy for mortals. Athena (goddess of wisdom, among other things) produced an olive tree, symbol of peace and prosperity. Poseidon (god of the sea) struck a rock with his trident, creating a saltwater spring, to signify great maritime power. It was a close contest, but the gods judged that Athena's gift, which would provide food, oil and fuel, would better serve the citizens – though of course Athens today draws its wealth from Poseidon's domain as well.

Building the Acropolis

The Acropolis was first inhabited in Neolithic times (4000–3000 BCE). The earliest temples were built during the Mycenaean era, in homage to the goddess Athena. People lived on the Acropolis until the late 6th century BCE, but in 510 BCE the Delphic oracle declared it the sole province of the gods.

After all the buildings on the Acropolis were reduced to ashes by the Persians on the eve of the Battle of Salamis (480 BCE), Pericles set about his ambitious rebuilding program. He transformed the Acropolis into a city of temples, which has come to be regarded as the zenith of Classical Greece. He spared no expense – only the best materials, architects, sculptors and artists were good enough for a city dedicated to the cult of Athena. It was a showcase of lavishly coloured buildings and gargantuan statues, some of bronze, others of marble plated with gold and encrusted with precious stones.

Preserving the Site

Foreign occupation, inept renovations, visitors' footsteps, earthquakes and, more recently, acid rain and pollution have all taken their toll on the surviving monuments. The worst blow was in 1687, when the Venetians attacked the Turks, opening fire on the Acropolis and causing an explosion in the Parthenon – where the Turks had been storing gunpowder – and damaging all the buildings. And in 1801, Thomas Bruse, Earl of Elgin, spirited away a portion of the Parthenon frieze, which is still on display in the British Museum, despite Greece's ongoing campaign for its return.

The Acropolis became a World Heritage–listed site in 1987. Major restoration programs are ongoing. Most of the original sculptures and friezes have been moved to the Acropolis Museum, so what you see now on the hill are replicas.

Odeon of Herodes Atticus

levels to compensate for the uneven bedrock.

Porch of the Caryatids

The Erechtheion is immediately recognisable by the six majestic maiden columns, the Caryatids (415 BCE), that support its southern portico. Modelled on women from Karyai (modern-day Karyes, in Lakonia), each figure is thought to have held a libation bowl in one hand, and to be drawing up her dress with the other. Those you see are plaster casts. The originals (except for one now in the British Museum) are in the Acropolis Museum.

Themistocles' Wall

Crafty general Themistocles (524–459 BCE) hastened to build a protective wall around the Acropolis and in so doing incorporated elements from archaic temples on

the site. When you're down the hill in Monastiraki, look for the column drums built into the wall on the north side of the Erechtheion.

Propylaia

The monumental entrance to the Acropolis, the Propylaia was built by Mnesicles between 437 BCE and 432 BCE and consists of a central hall with two wings on either side. In ancient times its five gates were the only entrances to the 'upper city'. The middle gate opens onto the Panathenaic Way. The ceiling of the central hall was painted with gold stars on a dark-blue background. The northern wing was used as a *pinakothiki* (art gallery).

Temple of Athena Nike

Recently restored, this exquisitely proportioned tiny Pentelic marble temple was designed by Kallicrates and built around 425 BCE. The internal cella housed a wooden statue of Athena as Victory (Nike) and the exterior friezes illustrated scenes from mythology, the Battle of Plataea (479 BCE) and Athenians fighting Boeotians and Persians. Parts of the frieze are in the Acropolis Museum, as are some relief sculptures, including the beautiful depiction of Athena Nike fastening her sandal.

Beulé Gate & Monument of Agrippa

Just outside the Propylaia lies the Beulé Gate, named after French archaeologist Ernest Beulé, who uncovered it in 1852. The 8m pedestal halfway up the zigzagging ramp to the Propylaia was once topped by the Monument of Agrippa. This bronze statue of the Roman general riding a chariot was erected in 27 BCE to commemorate victory in the Panathenaic Games.

Odeon of Herodes Atticus

The largest structure on the south slope is a magnificent ancient theatre, the Odeon of Herodes Atticus (p49), built in CE 161 and still in use. The path leads along the top edge; from this vantage the space looks positively intimate, though in fact it seats 5000 people.

Asclepion & Stoa of Eumenes

East of the odeon is the Asclepion, a temple built around a sacred spring. The worship of Asclepius, the physician son of Apollo, began in Epidavros and was introduced to Athens in 429 BCE at a time when plague was sweeping the city: people sought cures here.

Beneath the Asclepion, the Stoa of Eumenes is a colonnade built by Eumenes II, King of Pergamum (197–159 BCE), as a shelter and promenade for theatre audiences.

Theatre of Dionysos

The 6th-century-BCE timber theatre that stood here is thought to be the world's first. Reconstructed in stone and marble between 342 and 326 BCE, the theatre held 17,000 spectators (spread over 64 tiers, of which only about 20 survive) and an altar to Dionysos in the orchestra pit.

Thrones & Carvings

The ringside Pentelic marble thrones were for dignitaries and priests. The grandest, with lions' paws, satyrs and griffins, was reserved for the Priest of Dionysos. The 2nd-century-BCE reliefs at the rear of the stage depict the exploits of Dionysos.

Statues of hefty *selini* stood here too. These were worshippers of the mythical Selinos, the debauched father of the satyrs, whose favourite pastime was charging up mountains with his oversized phallus in lecherous pursuit of nymphs. The *selini* are in a sheltered area near the ticket booth for protection from the weather.

Top Experience 📷

Examine Treasures at the Acropolis Museum

The grand Acropolis Museum displays the surviving treasures from the temple hill, with emphasis on the Acropolis as it was in the 5th century BCE, the height of Greece's artistic achievement. The museum showcases layers of history: glass floors expose subterranean ruins, and the Acropolis is visible through the floor-to-ceiling windows, so the masterpieces are always in context.

◉ MAP P42, C3

www.theacropolis
museum.gr

adult/child €5/free

🕐 8am-4pm Mon, to 8pm Tue-Sun, to 10pm Fri Apr-Oct, 9am-5pm Mon-Thu, to 10pm Fri, to 8pm Sat & Sun Nov-Mar

Ⓜ Akropoli

Foyer Gallery

Finds from the slopes of the Acropolis fill the entry, where the floor's slope echoes the climb up the sacred hill. Glass reveals the ruins beneath the museum foundation. Objects here include votive offerings from sanctuaries and, near the entrance, two clay statues of Nike.

Archaic Gallery

The 1st floor is a veritable forest of statues, including some stunning 6th-century *kore* (maiden) statues: young women in draped clothing and elaborate braids. Most were recovered from a pit on the Acropolis, where the Athenians buried them after the Battle of Salamis. The youth bearing a calf, from 570 BCE, is one of the rare male statues discovered.

Early Temple Treasures

The Archaic Gallery also houses bronze figurines and interesting finds from temples predating the Parthenon. These include elaborate pedimental sculptures of Heracles slaying the Lernaian Hydra and a lioness devouring a bull.

Caryatids

On the mezzanine of the 1st floor are the five grand Caryatids (pictured left), the world-famous maiden columns that held up the porch of the Erechtheion. (The sixth is in the British Museum.)

Parthenon Gallery

The museum's crowning glory, the top-floor glass atrium showcases the Parthenon's pediments, metopes and 160m frieze. When the museum opened in 2007, it marked the first time in more than 200 years that the frieze was displayed in sequence, depicting the full Panathenaic Procession. In between golden-hued originals are white plaster replicas of missing pieces – the controversial Parthenon Marbles taken to Britain by Lord Elgin in 1801.

★ Top Tips

○ Buy tickets online to skip the queue.

○ EU students and under-18s enter free; non-EU students and youth, plus EU citizens over 65, get reduced admission. Bring ID.

○ Leave time for the fine museum shop (ground floor) and the film describing the history of the Acropolis (top floor).

○ Last admission is 30 minutes before closing, and galleries are cleared 15 minutes before closing, starting at the top floor.

○ You can visit the restaurant on the top floor without paying; ask at the ticket desk.

✗ Take a Break

The museum's **cafe-restaurant** on the 2nd floor has superb views and surprisingly reasonable prices (mains €10 to €15). Eat inside or sip a coffee alfresco on the terrace. If you want cheaper eats, head for Mikro Politiko (p45) for souvlaki.

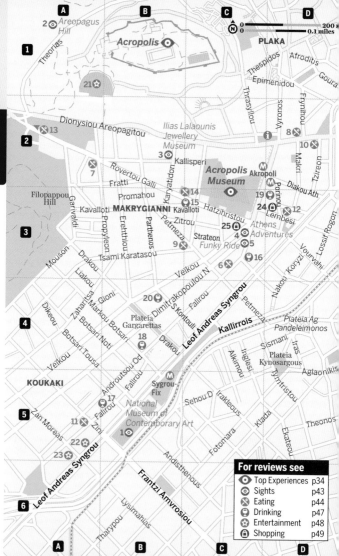

Acropolis Area

A **B** **C** **D**

1

2 Areopagus Hill

Acropolis

PLAKA

Theorias

Thespidos

Afroditis

Goura

Epimenidou

Thrasyllou

Frynihou

2

13

Dionysiou Areopagitou

Ilias Lalaounis Jewellery Museum

3 Kallisperi

Acropolis Museum

8

10

Akropoli

Vyronos

Makri

7

Rovertou Galli

Fratti

Karyatidon

Diakou Ath

Promahou

14

Pamou

19

Tziroen

Lossif Rogon

Filopappou Hill

Garivaldi

Kavalloti

MAKRYGIANNI Kavalloti

Hatzihristou

24

12

Erehthiou

Parthenos

Petmeza

Zitrou

25

Athens

Lembesi

Propyleon

Tsami Karatasou

15

Strateon

4

Adventures

3

9

Funky Ride 5

Nakou

Koryzi

Vourvahi

Mouson

Drakou

Veikou

6

16

Liakou

Dimitrakopoulou N

Petmeza

Kallirrois

Plateia Ag Pandeleimonos

Gioni

20

Falirou

Leof Andreas Syngrou

4

Zaharitsa

Markou Botsari

Plateia Gargarettas

S Kontouli

Drakou

Sismani

Iras

Plateia Kynosargous

Dikeou

Botsari Noti

18

Inglesi

Alkimou

Aglaonikis

Botsari Tousa

Androutsou Od

Falirou

Sygrou-Fix

Sehou D

Irakleous

Tymfristou

Theonos

KOUKAKI

Veikou

17

Falirou

Zini

National Museum of Contemporary Art

Klada

Fotomara

Ekateou

Zan Moras

11

1

Andisthenous

5

22

23

Leof Andreas Syngrou

Frantzi Amvrosiou

Tharypou

Lysimahias

6

A **B** **C** **D**

N
0   200 m
0   0.1 miles

For reviews see	
⊙ Top Experiences	p34
⊙ Sights	p43
⊗ Eating	p44
⊖ Drinking	p47
⊛ Entertainment	p48
⊕ Shopping	p49

Sights

National Museum of Contemporary Art
MUSEUM

1 ◎ MAP P42, B5

Set in the former Fix Brewery, the city's most prestigious contemporary museum opened in 2015. It exhibits Greek and international art in all media, from painting to video to experimental architecture. Shows can be hit or miss, and the building layout is not very welcoming, but when it's good, it's very good. (EMST; 📞 211 101 9000; www.emst.gr; Kallirrois & Frantzi, Koukaki-Syngrou; adult/student/child €4/2/free; ⏰ 11am-7pm Tue-Sun; Ⓜ Sygrou-Fix)

Areopagus Hill
PARK

2 ◎ MAP P42, A1

This rocky outcrop below the Acropolis has great views over the Ancient Agora. According to mythology, it was here that Ares was tried by the council of the gods for the murder of Halirrhothios, son of Poseidon. The council accepted his defence of justifiable deicide on the grounds that he was protecting his daughter, Alcippe, from unwanted advances. (Ⓜ Monastiraki)

Ilias Lalaounis Jewellery Museum
MUSEUM

3 ◎ MAP P42, B2

A museum for fashionistas: Ilias Lalaounis adorned Elizabeth Taylor and Melina Mercouri, among many others, and is responsible for a

Areopagus Hill

Capture the Flag

The one modern detail on the Acropolis (aside from the ever-present scaffolding and cranes) is the large Greek flag at the far east end. In 1941, early in the Nazi occupation, two teenage boys climbed up the cliff and raised the Greek flag; their act of resistance is commemorated on a brass plaque nearby.

singularly Greek style of bold, classically inspired gold jewellery. This museum shows all his work, which draws on everything from Greek wildflowers to pre-Columbian motifs. There's a hands-on jewellery studio on the ground floor, as well as a small gift shop. (☑ 210 922 1044; www.lalaounis-jewelrymuseum.gr; Kallisperi 12, cnr Karyatidon, Makrygianni; adult/child €5/free; ☺ 9am-3pm Tue-Sat, 11am-4pm Sun; Ⓜ Akropoli)

Athens Adventures   TOURS

4 ◉ MAP P42, C3

Run by the team from the popular Athens Backpackers hostel, this group offers a very popular Athens walking tour (€7; 10am Monday to Saturday), no reservation needed. (☑ 210 922 4044; www.athens adventures.gr; Veïkou 3a, Makrygianni; Ⓜ Akropoli)

Funky Ride   CYCLING

5 ◉ MAP P42, C3

Riding a rental bike around the Acropolis area is a good way to see the sights and catch a breeze. (☑ 211 710 9366; www.funkyride.gr; Dimitrakopoulou 1, Koukaki; 3hr/day €7/15; Ⓜ Akropoli)

Eating

Mani Mani   GREEK €€

6 ✕ MAP P42, C3

Head upstairs to the relaxing, elegant dining rooms of this delightful modern restaurant, which specialises in herb-filled cuisine from the Mani region in the Peloponnese. Standouts include the ravioli with Swiss chard and the tangy sausage with orange. (☑ 210 921 8180; www.manimani.com.gr/english.html; Falirou 10, Makrygianni; mains €15-20; ☺ 2-11pm Mon-Sat, 1-6pm Sun; Ⓜ Akropoli)

Strofi   GREEK €€

7 ✕ MAP P42, A2

Book ahead for a Parthenon view from the rooftop of this exquisitely renovated townhouse. Food is simple grilled meats and fish, but the setting, with elegant white linen and excellent service, elevates the experience to romantic levels. (☑ 210 921 4130; www.strofi.gr; Rovertou Galli 25, Makrygianni; mains €11-15; ☺ noon-1am, closed Mon Nov-Apr; Ⓜ Akropoli)

Mikro Politiko FAST FOOD €

8 🍴 MAP P42, D2

Just the thing to stave off post-Acropolis collapse: a quick souvlaki or falafel from this little place. It's markedly better than other snack options in the area, with fresh ingredients and good salads too. There are benches out front, or the pleasant staff can pack food to go. (📞210 321 7879; Dionysiou Areopagitou 8, Makrygianni; souvlaki €1.70; ⏰11am-midnight; Ⓜ Akropoli)

Lotte Cafe-Bistrot CAFE €

9 🍴 MAP P42, B3

Hide away from central Athens noise at this small, just-this-side-of-twee cafe. Sit outside in a private-feeling patch of tree-covered sidewalk, or inside amid vintage books and tea sets. Food is homemade cakes and light snacks. (📞211 407 8639; Tsami Karatsou 2, Makrygianni; snacks €2.50-7; ⏰9am-2am; Ⓜ Akropoli)

Fresko Yogurt Bar DESSERTS €

10 🍴 MAP P42, D2

Delicious Greek yoghurt is the base of all things here. Either fresh or in smoothie form, you can pair it with any number of toppings, from chocolate to black-cherry spoon sweets. A perfect cool-off after seeing the Acropolis. (📞210 923 3760; www.freskoyogurtbar.gr; Dionysiou Areopagitou 3, Makrygianni; yoghurt from €2.20; ⏰9am-9pm; Ⓜ Akropoli)

Greek food

Dream Homes

The mansions along Dionysiou Areopagitou, and in the blocks just behind, are some of the most coveted real estate in the city. At the intersection with Parthenos, note the outline of a building foundation – it marks the remains of a Roman villa now covered by the street.

Fabrika tou Efrosinou GREEK €€

11 MAP P42, A5

Named for the patron saint of cooks, this 'factory' is really a two-level restaurant focusing on good ingredients and rarer Greek recipes. Service can be a little patchy (all those stairs), but when everything is swinging, it's the perfect combination of bountiful, healthy food, excellent wine (a co-owner is a winemaker) and great atmosphere. Book ahead on weekends. (Zini 34, Koukaki; mains €8-17; 1.30-11pm Tue-Thu, to midnight Fri & Sat, 1-10pm Sun; M Sygrou-Fix, Fix)

Aglio, Olio & Peperoncino ITALIAN €€

12 MAP P42, D3

The food at this cosy Italian trattoria is simple pastas and the like, satisfying and reasonably priced. It's enhanced by the satisfaction of evading all the restaurant touts facing the nearby Acropolis Museum and finding this place on a quiet side street. (210 921 1801;

Porinou 13, Makrygianni; mains €15-25; 6pm-midnight Tue-Sat, 2-7pm Sun; M Akropoli)

Dionysos MEDITERRANEAN €€€

13 MAP P42, A2

Directly across from the Acropolis main entrance, this is ground zero for tour-bus lunches. But you could do a lot worse if you're in need of a restorative coffee, and in the evening, when the big groups move out, upper-level tables have a clear view of the south slope of the Acropolis. Food is pricey but good, and service is attentive. (210 923 1936; www.dionysos zonars.gr; Rovertou Galli 43, Makrygianni; mains €19-36; restaurant noon-1am, cafe 8am-1am; M Akropoli)

Point a MEDITERRANEAN €€

14 MAP P42, C3

The rooftop restaurant of the **Herodion Hotel** (www.herodion.gr), with stunning Acropolis and Acropolis Museum views, serves guests and loyal locals alike. Signature 'tapas cocktails' are served with a savoury appetiser, like the honey-topped *loukoumadhes* (doughnuts) filled with Elassona *manouri* cheese. Dishes are a creative presentation of traditional Mediterranean and Greek specialities such as the tender *sofrito* (traditional veal dish from Corfu). (210 923 6832; www.acropolispoint.com; Rovertou Galli 4a; mains €15-24; 7pm-midnight Jun-Oct; M Akropoli)

Drinking

Little Tree Book Cafe CAFE

15 MAP P42, C3

This friendly social hub is much beloved by neighbourhood residents, who go for books, but also excellent coffee, cocktails and snacks. (☎210 924 3762; www.facebook.com/littletreebooksandcoffee; Kavalloti 2, Makrygianni; ⏰8am-11pm Tue-Fri, 9am-11.30pm Sat & Sun; Ⓜ Akropoli)

Tiki Athens BAR

16 MAP P42, C3

Kitschy bachelor-pad decor, a whole roster of live music, an Asian-inspired menu and an alternative young crowd make this two-storey spot a fun place for a drink. (☎210 923 6908; www.tikiathens.com; Falirou 15, Makrygianni; ⏰11am-3am, to 4pm Fri & Sat, to 2am Sun; Ⓜ Akropoli)

Materia Prima WINE BAR

17 MAP P42, B5

Forget your normal image of a wine bar: Materia Prima is all light and air and blond wood, with an almost hippie dedication to artisan winemaking, in Greece and beyond. (☎210 924 5935; www.materiaprima.gr; Falirou 68, Koukaki; ⏰5pm-1am; Ⓜ Sygrou-Fix)

Kinono CAFE

18 MAP P42, B4

This airy modern cafe-bar is all blond wood and industrial fittings, softened with orchids and homey touches like a daily soup special. It's one of several good cafes all in a row, on either side of Falirou. (☎211 408 6826; Falirou 48, Koukaki; ⏰10am-2am, to 3.15am Fri & Sat; 🛜; Ⓜ Sygrou-Fix)

Hitchcocktales COCKTAIL BAR

19 MAP P42, D3

Famous Hitchcock film scenes are spray-painted on the wall in front of this bar on a quiet street with pillows out front for lounging. The bartenders are polished, and the soundtrack is usually lively swing, jazz, soul and funk. But the noise level, in the industrial-look raw-concrete space, can spike later in the night. (☎210 921 0023; www.facebook.com/hitchcock.athens; Porinou 10; ⏰5pm-4am; Ⓜ Acropolis)

Local Restaurant Row

Drakou between Veïkou and Leoforos Syngrou is a tree-shaded pedestrian street dotted with bars and cafes. While no single place excels, it's a good destination when you just want to be out of the tourist fray.

Sfika
BAR

20 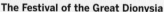 MAP P42, B4

Glowing yellow inside (perhaps for its namesake; *sfika* means 'wasp'), this small neighbourhood cafe-restaurant-bar has an alternative/student vibe and occasional live music. (📞210 922 1341; Stratigou Kontouli 15, Makrygianni; ⏰11am-2am; Ⓜ️Akropoli)

Entertainment

Odeon of Herodes Atticus
THEATRE

21 ⭐ MAP P42, A1

This large amphitheatre was built in CE 161 by wealthy Roman Herodes Atticus in memory of his wife Regilla. It was excavated in 1857–58 and completely restored

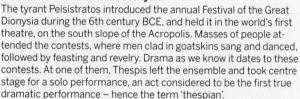

Athens: Birthplace of Theatre

The Festival of the Great Dionysia

The tyrant Peisistratos introduced the annual Festival of the Great Dionysia during the 6th century BCE, and held it in the world's first theatre, on the south slope of the Acropolis. Masses of people attended the contests, where men clad in goatskins sang and danced, followed by feasting and revelry. Drama as we know it dates to these contests. At one of them, Thespis left the ensemble and took centre stage for a solo performance, an act considered to be the first true dramatic performance – hence the term 'thespian'.

Drama in the Golden Age

During the golden age in the 5th century BCE, the annual festival was one of the state's major events. Politicians sponsored dramas by writers such as Aeschylus, Sophocles and Euripides, with some light relief provided by the bawdy comedies of Aristophanes. People came from all over Attica, with their expenses met by the state.

Greek Theatre Today

Athens continues to support an excellent theatre scene. The works of the classical Greek playwrights are still performed regularly, most notably during the summer Athens & Epidaurus Festival (p20), which stages the classics (and more contemporary works) at the Odeon of Herodes Atticus and the stunningly preserved theatre in Epidavros in the Peloponnese.

In winter, Athens' 200-plus theatres present everything from Sophocles to Beckett to works by contemporary Greek playwrights. The National Theatre (p143) is the best place to catch shows with English surtitles.

in the 1950s. The Athens & Epidaurus Festival (p20) holds drama, music and dance performances here in summer, and occasionally there are blockbuster pop concerts. (Herodeon; ☎ 210 324 1807; Ⓜ Akropoli)

Mikrokosmos

CINEMA

22 ⭐ MAP P42, A5

Why leave all the film fun to the outdoor cinemas? This great art-house theatre has comfy plush seats and a really nice bar. (☎ 210 923 0081; www.facebook.com/mikrokosmoscinema; Leoforos Syngrou 106, Koukaki; adult/child €7/5; Ⓜ Sygrou-Fix)

Koukles

LIVE PERFORMANCE

23 ⭐ MAP P42, A5

The glam drag show here is as kitschy as you'd hope. (☎ 694 755 7443; Zan Moreas 32, Koukaki; ☉ midnight-4am; Ⓜ Sygrou-Fix)

Shopping

El.Marneri Galerie

JEWELLERY, ART

24 🔒 MAP P42, D3

Sample rotating exhibitions of local modern art and some of the best jewellery in the city. Handmade, unusual and totally eye-catching. (☎ 210 861 9488;

Dionysiou Areopagitou St

APOSTOLIS GIONTZIS/SHUTTERSTOCK ©

www.elenimarneri.com; Lembesi 5-7, Makrygianni; ☉ 11am-8pm Tue, Thu & Fri, to 4pm Wed & Sat; Ⓜ Akropoli)

Lovecuts

CLOTHING

25 🔒 MAP P42, C3

A young Greek designer makes all the cute, affordable cotton clothing here, such as reversible hoodies and skirts in fun prints. One of several creative, small-scale boutiques on this street. (☎ 215 501 1526; Veïkou 2, Makrygianni; ☉ 10am-5pm Mon & Wed, 10am-2.30pm & 5.15-8.30pm Tue, Thu & Fri, 10am-3pm Sat, 11am-4pm Sun; Ⓜ Akropoli)

Walking Tour 🥾

Ancient Athens

The key ancient sites of Athens make for an action-packed but manageable walk, from the Temple of Olympian Zeus, past the Acropolis Museum and up to the Acropolis, then down around the other side of the hallowed hill into the Plaka and Monastiraki neighbourhoods, where you will find the Ancient Agora and Roman Agora. If you have only one day to see the sights, this is the walk to take.

Walk Facts

Start Temple of Olympian Zeus; metro Akropoli

Finish Ancient Agora; metro Monastiraki, Thisio

Length 2.4km; 3.5 hours

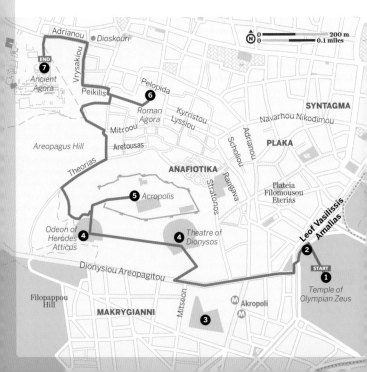

❶ Temple of Olympian Zeus

The striking **Temple of Olympian Zeus** (p116), the largest temple in Greece, had 104 Corinthian columns, of which 15 remain. Construction began in the 6th century BCE, and Hadrian finally completed it in CE 131.

❷ Hadrian's Arch

Teetering on the edge of traffic, **Hadrian's Arch** (cnr Leoforos Vasilissis Olgas & Leoforos Vasilissis Amalias; admission free; M Akropoli, Syntagma) is the ornate gateway erected in CE 132 to mark the boundary between Hadrian's new monuments and the ancient city.

❸ Acropolis Museum

The landmark **Acropolis Museum** (p40) displays the precious sculptures from the Acropolis. These include the caryatids and amazing works from the Parthenon's pediments, metopes and frieze.

❹ Ancient Theatres

Enter the Acropolis area via the eastern gate and, on the way up the southern slope of the Acropolis, explore the **Theatre of Dionysos** (p39) – the birthplace of theatre – and the magnificent **Odeon of Herodes Atticus** (p49), built in CE 161 and still in use today.

❺ Acropolis

The **Acropolis** (p34) is the most important ancient site in the Western world. Take in its diminu-

tive, restored Temple of Athena Nike, then enter through the grand gates of the Propylaia to visit the iconic Parthenon as well as the Erechtheion, edged with caryatids, the embodiment of 'statuesque'. On a clear day you can see for miles from the hilltop.

❻ Roman Agora

Exit the Acropolis from the west gate and walk down to Athens' 2nd-century commercial centre: the **Roman Agora** (p62). The highlight is the well-preserved **Tower of the Winds** (p62). Built in the 1st century BCE, it functioned as an ingenious sundial, weather vane and water clock.

❼ Ancient Agora

The **Ancient Agora** (p54) was the seat of democracy, philosophy and commerce. This rambling site, with the superb Temple of Hephaistos, also has a top-notch museum in the colonnaded Stoa of Attalos.

✕ Take a Break

Two of the easiest spots to stop are the Acropolis Museum's restaurant, with its magical views of the Parthenon, and **Dioskouri** (p67), among the many good options on Adrianou, near the Ancient Agora, for traditional Greek snacks.

Explore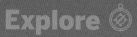
Monastiraki & Psyrri

Monastiraki is where Athens' history stacks up: on the main square is a 10th-century church (built as a monastery; hence the name) and the Ottoman-era Mosque of Tzistarakis – and then the Acropolis rises behind both. Psyrri, by contrast, has good contemporary art galleries and great street art. Some blocks might look dilapidated, but it's the city's liveliest quarter, where restaurants and bars coexist with warehouse conversions and workshops.

Start the day at the large Ancient Agora (p54); allow about an hour and a half. Then walk by the smaller Roman Agora (p62), and pop inside if you're interested in the vestiges of Athens' Ottoman period that form a second layer of history. Lunch break on Adrianou, or head up to Psyrri and casual seafood at Atlantikos (p68). Then cruise the Monastiraki flea market, with a coffee break at Orea Hellas (p69). Hear great local music with dinner at Akordeon (p67), or go for people-watching and kebab at Thanasis (p66). After that, bars galore: Six d.o.g.s. (p69), Noel (p70) and plenty more.

Getting There & Around

🅼 Monastiraki station (blue and green lines) is the most central stop.

🅼 Thissio (green line) is also convenient for Psyrri.

🅼 Omonia (green and red lines) is closest to the central market and the north part of Psyrri.

Neighbourhood Map on p60

Temple of Hephaistos (p55) WESTEND61/GETTY IMAGES ©

Top Experience 📸

Step into the Past at the Ancient Agora

Starting in the 6th century BCE, this area was Athens' commercial, political and social hub. Socrates expounded his philosophy here, and St Paul preached here. The site today has been cleared of later Ottoman buildings to reveal only classical remains. It's a green respite, with a well-restored temple, a good museum and a Byzantine church.

◉ MAP P60, D5

http://odysseus.culture.gr

Adrianou 24, Monastiraki

adult/student/child €8/4/free

🕐 8am-8pm May-Oct, to 3pm Nov-Apr

Ⓜ Monastiraki

Stoa of Attalos

In architectural terms, a stoa is a covered portico, but the ancient model, this stoa built by King Attalos II of Pergamum (159–138 BCE), was essentially an ancient shopping mall. The majestic two-storey structure, with an open-front ground floor supported by 45 Doric columns, was filled with storefronts. (Today, Greek still uses the word *stoa* for a shopping arcade.) The building, which was restored in the 1950s, holds the site museum.

Agora Museum

At research time, the upper storey of the Stoa of Attalos was closed, making the ground floor of the museum uncomfortably crowded when tour groups cycle through. If you can work around the crowds, you'll find some beautiful sculpture (look for the bronze head of Nike, with inlaid eyes) and neat relics that show how the agora was used on a daily basis: ancient stone voting machines, coins, terracotta figurines and more. Some of the oldest finds date from 4000 BCE.

Ostraka

On display among the relics of daily life are *ostraka* (pottery sherds marked with names). These were the 'ballots' by which troublesome citizens were voted out of Athens for a period of 10 years – whence the word 'ostracized'. Many sherds here bear the name of Themistocles, a successful 5th-century-BCE ruler whose ambition eventually got him ousted. And one is marked 'Pericles', showing that the leader who established the Athenian empire was not immune from criticism (though he never received enough votes to be ostracized).

Temple of Hephaistos

On the opposite (west) end of the agora site stands the best-preserved Doric temple in

★ Top Tips

o The main (and most reliable) entrance is on Adrianou; the south entrance is open only at peak times.

o The Temple of Hephaistos is a key photo op: it's well-preserved, and you can get quite close to it.

o Site clearing starts 30 minutes before closing, from each end. Late in the day, visit the Temple of Hephaistos and the Stoa of Attalos first, then more central spots.

o If you're interested in birds, come early: the many trees here harbour a lot of life.

o Hours change. Call ahead to check.

✕ Take a Break

The site of the Agora today is itself a nice break from congested city streets. To sit a spell after a tour, visit the cafes and restaurants on Adrianou, where you can enjoy a coffee or a meal at Kuzina (p69) or Dioskouri (p67).

Greece. Built in 449 BCE by Iktinos, one of the architects of the Parthenon, it was dedicated to the god of the forge and surrounded by foundries and metalwork shops. It has 34 columns and a frieze on the eastern side depicting nine of the Twelve Labours of Hercules. In CE 1300 it was converted into the Church of Agios Georgios, then deconsecrated in 1934. In 1922 and 1923 it was a shelter for refugees from Asia Minor; iconic photos from that period show families hanging laundry among the pillars.

Stoa Foundations

Northeast of the Temple of Hephaistos are the foundations of the Stoa of Zeus Eleutherios, one of the places where Socrates spoke. Further north are the foundations of the Stoa of Basileios, as well as the Stoa Poikile, or 'Painted Stoa', for its murals of battles of myth and history, rendered by the leading artists of the day.

Council House & Tholos

Southeast of the Temple of Hephaistos, archaeologists uncovered the New Bouleuterion (Council House), where the Senate (originally created by Solon) met, while the heads of government met to the south at the circular Tholos.

Church of the Holy Apostles

This charming little Byzantine church (pictured p54), near the southern site gate, was built in the early 10th century to commemorate

The Great Panathenaic Festival

The biggest event in ancient Athens was the Panathenaic Procession, the climax of the Panathenaic Festival held to venerate the goddess Athena. The route cut through the whole city, including the Ancient Agora. Scenes of the procession are vividly depicted in the 160m-long Parthenon frieze in the Acropolis Museum (p40).

The Contests

There were actually two festivals, a relatively sedate annual one to mark Athena's birthdate, approximately in July, and a grander one every fourth year. This Great Panathenaic Festival began with dancing, followed by athletic, dramatic and musical contests. Starting in the 4th century BCE, the Panathenaic Stadium (p120) hosted many of the athletic events, which included a pentathlon (footracing, discus and javelin throwing, long jump and wrestling), chariot races and the free-fighting match called pankration. Winners were presented with amphorae (vase-shaped ceramic vessels) containing oil from Athens' sacred olive trees; some of these are on display in the National Archaeological Museum (p128).

The Panathenaic Procession

On the final day of the festival, the Panathenaic Procession began at the Dipylon Gate of Kerameikos (p158), led by men carrying animals sacrificed to Athena, followed by maidens carrying *rhytons* (horn-shaped drinking vessels) and musicians playing a fanfare for the girls of noble birth who held aloft the sacred *peplos* (a glorious saffron-coloured shawl). During the preceding year, this select group of young women wove the *peplos* for the festival – a great honour.

The parade followed the Panathenaic Way, which cuts across the Ancient Agora and the middle of the Acropolis. Not everyone was allowed to enter the Acropolis, but in the festival's grande finale, the favoured few ultimately placed the *peplos* on the statue of Athena Polias in the Erechtheion.

St Paul's teaching in the Agora. Following the style of the time, its external brick decorations mimic Arabic calligraphy. During the period of Ottoman rule, it underwent many changes, but between 1954 and 1957 it was stripped of its 19th-century additions and restored to its original form. It contains several fine Byzantine frescoes, which were transferred from a demolished church.

Walking Tour 🚶

Commerce in Monastiraki & Psyrri

Emerging at Monastiraki station, you step right into Athens' vibrant character – the Acropolis above, souvlaki aromas wafting from Mitropoleos, fruit vendors hawking the best of the season and pedestrian lanes lined with enticing shops. If you can, come on a Sunday morning for the flea market, and stay into the afternoon for mezedhes and music at local cafes.

Walk Facts

Start Plateia Avyssinias

Finish Protogenous at Athinas

Length 1km; one hour

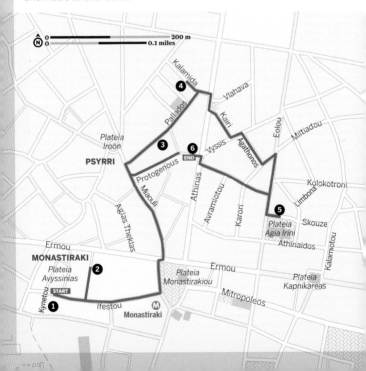

❶ Monastiraki Flea Market

Ifestou is signed as the 'Athens flea market', but it's mostly souvenir shops. The true flea feel is on **Plateia Avyssinias** (☉daily May-Oct, Sun-Wed & Fri Nov-Apr; Ⓜ Monastiraki), where dusty *palaiopoleia* ('old-stuff sellers') rule. The best rummaging is Sundays, when additional vendors lay out wares along Astingos and other nearby blocks.

❷ One-Stop Shopping

A few multi-use spaces in Psyrri and Monastiraki merge gallery, cafe and bar. One popular place is **TAF** (p64), which has a garden courtyard for drinks and a high-design souvenir shop.

❸ Pallados & Protogenous Streets

These eclectic shopping streets mix traditional (rope dealers, handmade baskets) and contemporary goods, as at cool basement shop **Color Skates** (☎210 331 7119; www.colorskates.com; Protogenous 5, Psyrri; ☉11am-7pm Mon, Wed & Sat, to 9pm Tue, Thu & Fri, noon-6pm Sun), where Athenians get their decks, and **AD Gallery** (Alpha Delta; ☎210 322 8785; www.adgallery.gr; Pallados 3, 2nd fl, Psyrri; ☉noon-9pm Tue-Fri, to 4pm Sat Sep-Jul), home to cutting-edge contemporary Greek artists.

❹ Equestrian Crafts

Of all of Psyrri's niche old shopping districts, the donkey-decoration district might be the niche-est. At tiny **Hrisanthos** (☎210 323 7584; Kalamida 3, Psyrri), shop for beaded bridles and shepherd bells – or, if you don't have a donkey, a set of worry beads. Just around the corner, chic **Mompso** (☎210 323 0670; www.mompso. com; Athinas 33, Psyrri; ☉10am-6pm Mon-Sat) is the upscale version, catering to Athens' horsey set.

❺ Top Souvlaki

When you get hungry, stroll down to pretty Plateia Agia Irini, to tiny **Kostas** (p65) and its excellent pork souvlaki. A lovely veg-friendly option a couple of blocks north is **Feyrouz** (www.feyrouz.gr; Karori 23; sandwiches from €3; ☉noon-10pm Mon-Thu, to 11pm Fri & Sat; 🌿), which does a delicious meatless *lahmajoun* (flatbread topped with spicy paste and filled with vegetables).

❻ A Sweet Finish

Backtrack for dessert at **Kokkion** (☎6981563511; Protogenous 2, Psyrri; scoop €2.50; ☉8am-midnight Mon-Fri, from 10am Sat & Sun, reduced hours in winter), a tiny ice-cream shop that does intense fruit flavours (ginger-mandarin, say) and very rich chocolates. There's also a full coffee operation, for an afternoon pick-me-up.

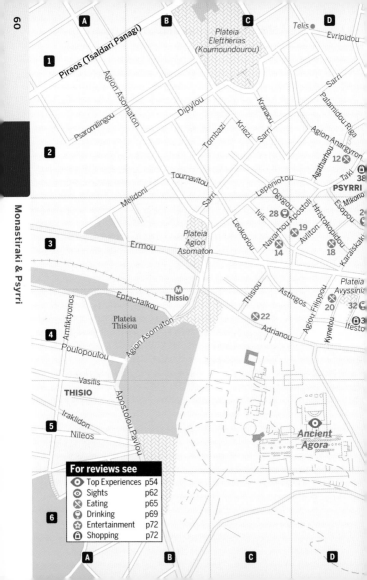

A | B | C | D

1

Pireos (Tsaldari Panagi)

Plateia
Eleftherias
(Koumoundourou)

Telis •

Evripidou

Agion Asomaton

Psaromilingou

Dipylou

Kranaou

Sarri

Palamidiou-Riga

2

Tombazi

Krezi

Sarri

Agion Anargyron

12 ✕

Taki

Tournavitou

Lepeniotou

38

PSYRRI

Melidoni

Sarri

Ogygou

28 ✕

Ivis

Navarhou Apostoli

Hristokopidou

Esopou

Mikono

24

3

Ermou

Plateia
Agion
Asomaton

Leokoriou

14

19 ✕

Avliton

18

Karaiskaki

Plateia
Avyssinia

Eptachalkou

M
Thissio

Thisiou

Astingos

Agiou Filippou

20

32

4

Plateia
Thisiou

Amfiktyonos

Agion Asomaton

Adrianou

22 ✕

Kynetou

Ifesto

3

Poulopoulou

Apostolou Pavlou

Vasilis

THISIO

5

Iraklidon

Nileos

Ancient
Agora

For reviews see
- ◉ Top Experiences p54
- ◉ Sights p62
- ✕ Eating p65
- 🍷 Drinking p69
- ★ Entertainment p72
- 🔒 Shopping p72

6

A | B | C | D

Aristogitonos
8
36
Athinas
Meat Market
Eolou
Evripidou
35
Eshylou
15
Agiou Dimitriou
Polykliitou
Hrysospiliotissis
Ag Markou
Praxitelous
Aristofanous
17
Plateia Iroon
Kodrika
Pallados
30
Protogenous
Vyssis
Agathonos
Eolou
Nikiou
42
Leoharous
11 10
Athinas
Voreou
Limbona
27 31
Kolokotroni
Klitiou
Agias Theklas
Miaouli
Avramiotou
23
Karori
9
Skouze
29
25
Romvis
Themidos
Agias Irinis
Plateia Agia Irini
33
Perikleous
40
A for Athens
Lukumades
Athinaidos
21
Couleur Locale
Ermou
6
Church of Kapnikarea
TAF
Plateia Monastirakiou
City Zen
Plateia Dimopratiriou
Kapnikareas
Plateia Kapnikareas
41
Normanou
13
39
Nisou
16
Monastiraki
24
37
Mitropoleos
Athens Cathedral
MONASTIRAKI
Mosque of Tzistarakis
Pandrosou
Plateia Mitropoleos
3
Adrianou
Areos
Hadrian's Library
Kalogrioni
Mnisikleous
Vlahou Ang
Church of Agios Eleftherios
4
Vrysakiou
Kladou
Dexippou
Plateia Arhaia Agoras
Adrianou
5
Peikilis
Epam/nonda
Eolou
Pelopida
Diogenous
PLAKA
1
Roman Agora
Tower of the Winds
2
Markou Aureliou
Bath House of the Winds
Agias Filotheis
Polygnotou
Dioskouron
Panos
Mitroou
Thrasyvoulou
Kyrristou
Lyssiou
Flessa

Sights

Roman Agora HISTORIC SITE

1 MAP P60, E5

This was the city's market area under Roman rule, and it occupied a much larger area than the current site borders. You can see a lot from outside the fence, but it's worth going in for a closer look at the well-preserved **Gate of Athena Archegetis**, the propylaeum (entrance gate) to the market, as well as an Ottoman mosque and the ingenious and beautiful Tower of the Winds, on the east side of the site.

The gate, formed by four Doric columns, was financed by Julius Caesar and erected sometime during the 1st century CE. To the right of the entry, look also for the outlines of what was a 68-seat public latrine. (📞 210 324 5220; http://odysseus.culture.gr; Dioskouron, Monastiraki; adult/student/child €6/3/free; 🕐8am-3pm Mon-Fri, to 5pm Sat & Sun, mosque from 10am; Ⓜ Monastiraki)

Tower of the Winds MONUMENT

2 MAP P60, F5

This Pentelic marble tower within the Roman Agora, likely built in the 2nd century BCE, is both beautiful and functional. Devised by Andronicus, a Macedonian astronomer, it is an ancient time-and-weather station. It is aligned with the four cardinal directions, so that each of its eight sides is a compass point, each illustrated with a figure representing the wind from that direction. Sundial markings are visible below the reliefs, and it was topped with a weather vane, probably a bronze figure of Triton.

Inside the tower are the workings of a water clock, which

Athens under Roman Rule

A portion of Greece was first taken into the Roman empire in 146 BCE. In 86 BCE Athens joined an ill-fated rebellion in Asia Minor staged by the king of the Black Sea region, Mithridates VI. In retribution, the Roman statesman Sulla invaded Athens and took off with its most valuable sculptures. As the province of Achaea, the Greek peninsula was officially under the auspices of Rome, but some major cities were granted limited self-rule.

It helped, too, that Romans revered Greek culture, so Athens retained its status as a centre of learning. Under the rule of Roman emperors Augustus, Nero and Hadrian, the city flourished. Hadrian considered the city his empire's cultural capital and invested in a library, temples and an aqueduct. A period of relative peace, the Pax Romana, lasted in Greece until the middle of the 3rd century CE.

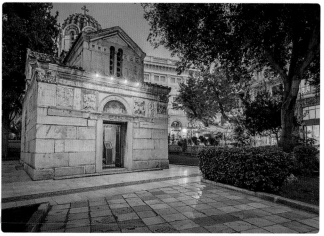

Church of Agios Eleftherios

marked time with water from a stream that flowed down from the Acropolis. The stone roof, one of very few preserved from ancient times, is 24 stone panels. Conservators have revealed patches of fresco – it was once painted all blue inside. There are also traces of later uses: a faint Roman drawing of a ship, a patch of a Byzantine angel fresco and Arabic calligraphy and a mihrab (prayer niche) from the late Ottoman period.

Athens Cathedral   CHURCH

3 ◉ MAP P60, H5

The ornate 1862 Athens Cathedral is the seat of the archbishop of the Greek Orthodox Church of Athens. However, far more significant, both historically and architectur-

ally, is the small, 12th-century, cruciform-style marble Church of Agios Eleftherios next to the cathedral, built of bits and pieces of ancient temples and earlier Christian monuments. (📞210 322 1308; Plateia Mitropoleos, Monastiraki; 🕓7am-7pm; Ⓜ Monastiraki)

Church of Agios Eleftherios   CHURCH

4 ◉ MAP P60, H5

This 12th-century church, known as the Little Metropolis and dedicated to both Agios Eleftherios and Panagia Gorgoepikoos (Virgin Swift to Hear), is Athens' religious history in one tiny building. The cruciform-style marble church was erected on the ruins of an ancient temple and its exterior is a mix of

Ottoman Athens

Athens was under Ottoman rule for several centuries, but very few buildings survive, as archaeologists have been more eager to dig up older relics beneath. The largest surviving structure is the **Mosque of Tzistarakis** (Map p60, F4; ☎210 324 2066; www.melt.gr; Areos 1, Monastiraki; Ⓜ Monastiraki), which has been towering over Plateia Monastirakiou since 1759. The Museum of Greek Folk Art maintains the building, but it has been closed since 2015. The same museum also restored the Bath House of the Winds (p85), a typical Ottoman hammam.

Just around the corner, the Roman Agora (p62) contains a 17th-century mosque (now an exhibit space), and the ancient Tower of the Winds (p62) was used by Turkish dervishes as a *tekke* (a Sufi place of worship). Adjoining the *tekke*, across the road north of the tower, was a Sufi madrasah, built in the 18th century. In the 19th century, its student cells made it useful as a jail. Much of the building was demolished to excavate Roman ruins beneath. Only the front gate remains, overgrown with greenery.

medieval beasts and ancient gods in bas-relief, with columns appropriated from older structures. It was once the city's cathedral, but now stands in the shadows of the much larger new cathedral. (Little Metropolis; Plateia Mitropoleos, Monastiraki; Ⓜ Monastiraki)

TAF   GALLERY

5 ◉ MAP P60, E4

Whether you want a refreshing drink or a shot of art or a clever design morsel, stop in at TAF, a just-barely-updated complex of 1870s brick buildings. The central courtyard is a cafe-bar that fills with an eclectic young crowd, and the surrounding rooms act as gal-

leries, DJ space and an excellent souvenir shop. Events are usually free. (The Art Foundation; ☎210 323 8757; www.theartfoundation.gr; Normanou 5, Monastiraki; ☺noon-9pm Mon-Sat, to 7pm Sun, cafe-bar open late; Ⓜ Monastiraki)

Church of Kapnikarea   CHURCH

6 ◉ MAP P60, G4

This small 11th-century structure stands smack in the middle of the Ermou shopping strip. It was saved from the bulldozers and restored by Athens University. Its dome is supported by four large Roman columns. (Ermou, Monastiraki; ☺8am-2pm Tue, Thu & Fri; Ⓜ Monastiraki, Syntagma)

Hadrian's Library

RUINS

7 ◉ MAP P60, F4

These are the remains of the largest structure erected by Hadrian, in the 2nd century CE. Not just a library, it also held music and lecture rooms. It was laid out as a typical Roman forum, with a pool in the centre of a courtyard bordered by 100 columns. The library's west wall, by the site entrance, has been restored. Beyond are only traces of the library, as well as two churches, built in the 7th and 12th centuries.

You can get a good sense of the library's grand scale from outside the fence, uphill on Dexippou. It essentially functioned as Athens' civic centre in Roman times, while the nearby Roman Agora was the market. Admission to the site is included with the Acropolis combo ticket (€30), which permits entry to the Acropolis and six other sites (including this one) within five days. (🗷 210 324 9350; http://odys seus.culture.gr; Areos 3, Monastiraki; adult/child €4/free; 🕑 8am-3pm; Ⓜ Monastiraki)

Eating

Karamanlidika tou Fani

GREEK €€

8 🍴 MAP P60, E1

At this modern-day *pastomage-ireio* (combo tavern-deli) tables are set alongside the deli cases, and staff offer tasty morsels while you're looking at the menu. Beyond the Greek cheeses and cured meats, there's good seafood, such as marinated anchovies, as well as rarer wines and craft beers. Service is excellent, as is the warm welcome from Fani herself. (🗷 210 325 4184; www.karamanlidika. gr; Sokratous 1, Psyrri; dishes €7-18; 🕑 11am-midnight; Ⓜ Monastiraki)

Kostas

GREEK €

9 🍴 MAP P60, G3

On a pleasant square opposite Agia Irini church, this old-style virtual hole-in-the wall joint grills up tasty souvlaki and *bifteki* (Greek-seasoned hamburger), served on pita with a signature spicy tomato sauce. Go before the lunch rush, as it may close early if it runs out of meat. (🗷 210 323 2971; Plateia Agia Irini 2, Monastiraki; sandwich €2.20; 🕑 9am-6pm; Ⓜ Monastiraki)

Bougatsadiko I Thessaloniki

PIES €

10 🍴 MAP P60, E2

Unexpected for its location on a key nightlife square in Psyrri, this place makes excellent *pitta* (pies), with filo crust that's 'opened' (rolled out by hand) every day. *Bougatsa* (filo with custard) is great for breakfast, the meat pies are a treat after drinks and *spanakopita* (spinach pie) hits the spot anytime. (🗷 210 322 2088; Plateia Iroön 1, Psyrri; pita €2; 🕑 24hr; Ⓜ Monastiraki)

Pavement dining in Plateia Monastirakiou

Nancy's Sweethome · CAFE €

11  MAP P60, E2

Get your sugar fix at this place on a bustling square. It's famous for its extra-large cakes swimming in melted chocolate and giant dollops of ice cream. Also has syrup-soaked Greek pastries; a local favourite is the *kunefe*, a sweet cheese pastry served with a generous helping of mastic-flavoured ice cream. (210 321 1323; www.nancysweethome.gr; Plateia Iroön 1, Psyrri; cakes from €10; 8.30am-2.30am; Monastiraki)

Nikitas · TAVERNA €

12 MAP P60, D2

Locals swear by this tried-and-true taverna that has been serving rea-

sonably priced, refreshingly simple and tasty traditional food since well before Psyrri became a hot spot. It's the only place busy on weekdays. (210 325 2591; Agion Anargyron 19, Psyrri; mains €7-10; noon-6.30pm Sun-Tue, to 11.30pm Wed-Sat; Monastiraki)

Thanasis · KEBAB €

13 MAP P60, F4

In the heart of Athens' souvlaki hub, just off Plateia Monastirakiou, Thanasis is a good place to settle in and watch the street parade. It's known especially for its mince kebabs on pitta with grilled tomato and onions. (210 324 4705; Mitropoleos 69, Monastiraki; gyros €2.50; 8.30am-2.30am; Monastiraki)

Ivis

MEZEDHES €

14 ⊗ MAP P60, C3

This cosy corner place, with its bright, arty decor, has a small but delicious range of simple, freshly cooked mezedhes that change daily. A good ouzo and raki selection lights things up. (🗷 210 323 2554; Navarhou Apostoli 19, Psyrri; mezedhes €4-10; ⏱noon-2am Tue-Sat, to 8pm Sun; Ⓜ Thissio)

Avli

MEZEDHES €

15 ⊗ MAP P60, E1

Cheap, cheerful and borderline chaotic on weekend nights, Avli requires you to squeeze down a narrow hall to get in, and probably wait for service if it's busy. But the whitewashed walls and outdoor seating give you an island feel in the city, and the *keftedhes* (fried meatballs) and the special omelette, filled with fries and sausage, are excellent drinking food. (Agiou Dimitriou 12, Psyrri; dishes €5-10; ⏱1pm-midnight; Ⓜ Monastiraki)

Dioskouri

MEZEDHES €

16 ⊗ MAP P60, E4

This landmark cafe-restaurant sprawls over the road, overlooking the railway line. On the cafe side (Adrianou 39), tables sit under a huge shade tree that gives the place a traditional village feel. For coffee, ouzo and snacks, it's popular with students – and of course tourists, thanks to its location on this pedestrian street. (🗷 210 325 3333; www.dioskouriathens.gr;

Adrianou 37-39, Monastiraki; mezedhes €3-8; ⏱8.30am-1am; Ⓜ Monastiraki)

Taverna tou Psirri

TAVERNA €

17 ⊗ MAP P60, E2

This cheerful taverna just off Plateia Iroön turns out decent, no-frills traditional food. (🗷 210 321 4923; Eshylou 12, Psyrri; mains €6-9; ⏱noon-midnight, closed 2 weeks Aug; Ⓜ Monastiraki)

Akordeon

MEZEDHES €€

18 ⊗ MAP P60, D3

Slide into this charming butter-yellow house across from a church in a quiet Psyrri side street for a warm welcome by musician-chefs Pepi and Achilleas (and their spouses), who run this excellent venue for local music and

Snack Bonanza

Stand at the junction of Eolou and Athinaidos and look east and south for a delicious variety of snack food, from fresh falafel to fried fish. Then again, you might not make it past **Lukumades** (Map p60, G3; 🗷 210 321 0880; Eolou 21, Monastiraki; portion €2.70; ⏱8am-1am, to 3am Fri & Sat; Ⓜ Monastiraki), right on the corner, which serves *loukoumadhes*, Greece's excellent morsels of fried-dough, doused in traditional honey or filled with jam or ice cream.

Hot Grill

A fluorescent-lit beacon of good food and kind service on a grimy block, **Telis** (Map p60, D1; 210 324 2775; Evripidou 86, Psyrri; meal with salad €13; 8am-2am Mon-Sat; Thissio) has been serving up simplicity since 1978. There's no menu, just a set meal: a small mountain of charcoal-grilled pork chops atop chips, plus a side vegetable. Greek salad is optional, as is beer or rough house wine.

mezedhes. They'll help you order authentic Greek fare, then surround you with their soulful songs. (210 325 3703; Hristokopidou 7,

Grilled seafood

MATEUSZ GZIK/SHUTTERSTOCK ©

Psyrri; dishes €6-16; 7pm-1am Thu, to 2am Fri & Sat, 1-8pm Sun Sep-May; Monastiraki, Thissio)

Atlantikos   SEAFOOD €€

19 MAP P60, D3

Tucked down a little lane, this small, hip fish restaurant is easy to miss – look for happy people chatting over heaps of shrimp shells. The atmosphere is simple and casual, with low prices to match – but excellent quality seafood, whether it's fried or grilled. (213 033 0850; Avliton 7; mains €8-13; Monastiraki, Thissio)

Café Avyssinia   MEZEDHES €€

20 MAP P60, D4

This antiques-bedecked place on Plateia Avyssinias, in the middle of the antique dealers, has been legendary since the 1980s for its live music and varied mezedhes. But on a slow day it can feel a bit stuffy. Either take a midday break from the market, or go late on a weekend night. In summer, snag fantastic Acropolis views upstairs. (210 321 7047; Kynetou 7, Monastiraki; mains €10-16; 11am-1am Tue-Sat, to 7pm Sun; Monastiraki)

School Pizza Bar   ITALIAN €€

21 MAP P60, G3

Settle into a desk like the old days, and check out the chalkboard. Topping options for the thin-crust pizzas include good Greek products, such as cured pork from Crete. At night, it's the choice hang-out near trendy Plateia Agia Irini for excellent drinks and cocktails and lounge music by top local DJs. (210 325 1444; Plateia Agia Irini 8, Monastiraki; pizzas from €10; 10am-3am; M Monastiraki)

Kuzina
GREEK €€

22 MAP P60, C4

This comfortably elegant restaurant does chic Greek, with creations such as fried dumplings filled with feta and olives. It's cosy in winter, as light streams in, warming the crowded tables. In summer, book ahead for a rooftop-terrace table for views all around. A fine second choice is an outside table on the pedestrian street. (210 324 0133; www.kuzina.gr; Adrianou 9, Monastiraki; mains €12-25, set menu €22; 11am-late; M Thissio)

Drinking

Six d.o.g.s.
BAR

23 MAP P60, F3

The core of this supercreative events space is a rustic, multilevel back garden, a great place for quiet daytime chats over coffee or a relaxed drink. From there, you can head in to one of several adjoining buildings to see a band, art show or other general cool happening. (210 321 0510; www.sixdogs.gr; Avramiotou 6-8, Monastiraki; 10am-late; M Monastiraki)

Loukoumadhes

Orea Hellas
CAFE

24 MAP P60, F4

This lovely old-style coffee house is a perfect place to take a break from shopping on the Monastiraki strip. Head upstairs for a seat on an open balcony overlooking Mitropoleos, or, in cooler weather, an indoor spot with an Acropolis view. Pair your Greek coffee with sweets or a range of solid snacks and salads. The cafe also has a shop with excellent traditional craftwork from around the country. (210 321 3023; Pandrosou 36, Monastiraki; 9am-1am Apr-Oct, to 6pm Nov-Mar; ; M Monastiraki)

Dude
BAR

25 MAP P60, H3

Exceptionally good music – obscure funk and soul that makes

World's Best Views

Think 'Acropolis view' is just tourist bait? Think again: locals love these Monastiraki rooftop bars.

Couleur Locale (Map p60, E4; 216 700 4917; www.couleur localeathens.com; Normanou 3, Monastiraki; ⏱10am-2am Sun-Thu, to 3am Fri & Sat; M Monastiraki) The unsigned entrance is at the end of an arcade.

City Zen (Map p60, G4; 210 325 4942; www.facebook.com/ cityzenathens; Mitropoleos 80, Monastiraki; ⏱9am-4am; M Monastiraki) Less zen at night. Enter on Eolou.

A for Athens (Map p60, F3; 210 324 4244; www.aforath ens.com; Miaouli 2, Monastiraki; d from €190; ❄ 🛜; M Monastiraki) A big scene on the roof of this hotel.

you feel like you're living a Quentin Tarantino movie – plays at this little bar on a pedestrian street. What's more, the Dude buzzes till practically dawn. (210 322 7130; www.facebook.com/thedudebar; Kalamiotou 14, Monastiraki; ⏱12.30pm-5am Sun-Thu, to 6am Fri & Sat; M Monastiraki)

Little Kook   CAFE

26 🍺 MAP P60, D3

Nominally, this place sells coffee and cake. But it's really about its

dazzling decor, which conjures an odd childhood fantasy. Precisely which one depends on the season, as the theme changes regularly. Everywhere are dolls, props, paintings and table decorations. You'll know you're getting close when you see party streamers over the street. Kids will be dazzled; Instagrammers will swoon. (210 321 4144; www. facebook.com/littlekookgr; Karaïskaki 17, Psyrri; ⏱10am-midnight Mon-Fri, from 9am Sat & Sun; 🚼; M Monastiraki)

Noel   BAR

27 🍺 MAP P60, G3

The beautiful bar's slogan is 'where it's always Christmas' – meaning the candlelit cocktail-party kind of Christmas, no Santa suits required. Under softly glimmering chandeliers, smartly suited bartenders serve some of the most creative cocktails in town. Music is a mix of '80s, '90s and jazz. (211 215 9534; www.noelbar.gr; Kolokotroni 59b, Monastiraki; ⏱10am-2am Sun-Thu, to 4am Fri & Sat; M Monastiraki)

Spiti Mas   CAFE

28 🍺 MAP P60, C3

Fancy breakfast in bed? You can have it at 'Our House', a cafe set up like a hip apartment, complete with a single bed. The whole operation might be unbearably twee if it weren't for the good, fresh food and the genuinely sweet staff. (210 331 4751; Navarhou Apostoli 10, Psyrri; ⏱9am-4pm Mon & Wed-Fri, to 6pm Sat & Sun; M Thissio, Monastiraki)

Rooster CAFE

29 MAP P60, G3

This always-busy gay cafe on lively Plateia Agia Irini is straight-friendly, too. The atmosphere is great and quickly fills up with chatting locals. (☏ 210 322 4410; www.roostercafe.gr; Plateia Agia Irini 4, Monastiraki; ⊙9am-3am; 🛜; Ⓜ Monastiraki)

Tranzistor BAR

30 MAP P60, E2

Sidle up to the backlit bar or relax at tables outside at this small, cool spot. It's one of a few good mellow bars on this narrow street. (☏ 210 322 8658; Protogenous 10, Psyrri; ⊙9am-4am, from 11am Sun; Ⓜ Monastiraki)

Booze Cooperativa BAR

31 MAP P60, H3

By day this art mansion is full of young Athenians playing chess and working on their laptops. Later it turns into a lively bar that rocks till late. The basement hosts art exhibitions and there's a theatre upstairs. (☏ 211 405 3733; www.boozecoopera tiva.com; Kolokotroni 57, Monastiraki; ⊙11am-late; 🛜; Ⓜ Monastiraki)

Loukoumi CAFE

32 MAP P60, D4

This creative, gay-friendly cafe and arts space occupies two buildings facing each other across Plateia Avyssinias. It covers everything from daytime coffee to night-time DJs to drag queens, plus a vintage shop and gallery space. (☏ 210 323 4814; www.loukoumibar.gr; Plateia

Six d.o.g.s. (p69)

Avyssinias 3, Monastiraki; ⏰10am-3am Sun-Thu, to 4am Fri & Sat; Ⓜ Monastiraki)

Entertainment

Faust
CABARET

33 ⭐ MAP P60, G3

Loud, raunchy, funny, just plain quirky: eclectic and popular bar Faust probably hosts it on its small stage. The place closes in summer. (☎210 323 4095; www.faust.gr; Kalamiotou 11 & Athinaidos 12, Monastiraki; ⏰8pm-late Mon-Thu, from 5pm Fri-Sun, Sep-May; Ⓜ Monastiraki)

Shopping

Yiannis Samouelin
MUSIC

34 🅰 MAP P60, D4

Wedged between more modern, generic shops on Ifestou, this shop

Traditional Greek bouzouki

STF-MANAGEMENT/SHUTTERSTOCK ©

is the place to buy the bouzouki of your dreams. It has been dealing in musical instruments from around the world since 1928. (☎210 321 2433; www.musicshop.gr; Ifestou 36, Monastiraki; ⏰9am-7pm; Ⓜ Monastiraki)

Pan-Pol
HATS

35 🅰 MAP P60, F1

Whether you want a moss-green fedora or a non-touristy Greek fisherman's cap, this shoebox of a shop will have it, along with many other felt hats in lovely colours and classic shapes. Most of the stock comes from a workshop upstairs, and prices start at just €10. (☎210 321 1431; Athinas 36; ⏰10am-5pm Mon, Wed & Sat, to 7pm Tue, Thu & Fri; Ⓜ Monastiraki)

Big Bazaar
ANTIQUES

36 🅰 MAP P60, F1

The name of this junk shop is…an understatement. It's two floors and room upon room crammed with precariously balanced treasures, so many that it's difficult to process, much less pick through. Stash your bags on the ground floor, so you don't knock anything over by accident. (☎210 321 6565; Aristogitonos 9, Monastiraki; ⏰10am-6pm Mon-Sat; Ⓜ Omonia, Panepistimio)

Monastic Art Shop
HOMEWARES

37 🅰 MAP P60, G4

All of the products in this store are made by monks on Mt Athos: olives, wine, beauty products from wild and cultivated herbs, and beautiful gold and silver icons. (📞210 324 5034; Pandrosou 28; Ⓜ Syntagma, Monastiraki)

Kartousa
JEWELLERY, HOMEWARES

38 🅰 MAP P60, D2

Eclectic, folky handmade jewellery and homewares brighten this tiny storefront. (📞210 324 7525; Taki 9, Psyrri; ⏰11am-8pm Tue-Sat, noon-8pm Sun; Ⓜ Monastiraki)

Martinos
ANTIQUES

39 🅰 MAP P60, F4

This Monastiraki landmark opened in 1890 and has an excellent, often museum-quality selection of Greek and European antiques and collectables, including painted dowry chests, icons, coins, porcelain and furniture. (📞210 321 2414; www.martinosart.gr; Pandrosou 50, Monastiraki; ⏰10am-3pm Mon, Wed & Sat, to 6pm Tue, Thu & Fri, closed Sat Aug; Ⓜ Monastiraki)

Melissinos Art
SHOES

40 🅰 MAP P60, E3

On a lane with several shoemakers, Pantelis Melissinos continues the sandal-making tradition of his famous poet/cobbler father Stavros, who built his reputation crafting Classical-inspired shoes for Hollywood stars. The shop can get crowded, as people come for charming Pantelis himself. But the prices are reasonable – especially as the shoes are adjusted to your feet. (📞210 321 9247; www.melissino

Secondhand Style on Ermou

Smart Athenians like Monastiraki's junk shops for clothing too. There are several thrift stores on Ermou just across the road from Plateia Avyssinias.

spoetsandalmaker.com; Agias Theklas 2, Psyrri; ⏰10am-8pm, to 6pm winter; Ⓜ Monastiraki)

Olgianna Melissinos
SHOES

41 🅰 MAP P60, E4

Another scion of the legendary poet/sandal-maker Stavros Melissinos, Olgianna has a line of custom-fitted sandals as well as smart belts and bags. She can also make designs to order. (📞210 331 1925; www.melissinos-sandals.gr; Normanou 7, Monastiraki; ⏰10am-6pm Mon, Wed, Sat & Sun, to 8pm Tue, Thu & Fri; Ⓜ Monastiraki)

Shedia Home
ARTS & CRAFTS

42 🅰 MAP P60, G3

Shedia is Greece's version of street-vendor magazines such as the Big Issue. Unsold copies are upcycled into appealing homewares and accessories including papier-mâché lampshades and bowls, and dainty jewellery. The space beneath their editorial offices has been reimagined as a shop and stylish cafe-bar. (📞213 023 1220; www.shediahome.gr; Koloktroni 56, Monastiraki; ⏰10am-11.30pm; Ⓜ Monastiraki)

Walking Tour 🚶

Wandering the Central Market

The streets around the Athens Central Market (also referred to as the Varvakios Agora) are a sensory delight, all colour and bustle and noisy hawkers' cries. Some of the best, most traditional Athenian food experiences are found here, and you can also feast your eyes on art at some very good galleries nearby.

Walk Facts

Start Athinas at Evripidou

Finish Sarri

Length 1.3km; 1.5 hours

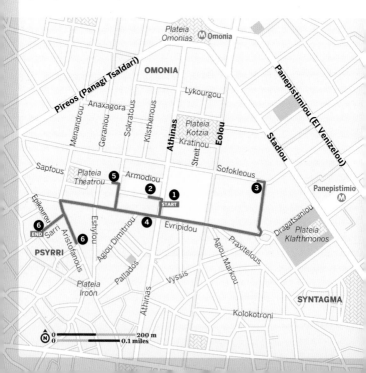

❶ Athens Central Market

A must for gastronomes, the historic **Varvakios Agora** (Athens Central Market; Athinas, btwn Sofokleous & Evripidou, Omonia; ⏰7am-6pm Mon-Sat; MⒷPanepistimio, Omonia) building contains the meat and seafood markets, packed with shiny-eyed fish and ruby-red lamb carcasses. (The vendors have rather famously resisted EU hygiene directives and still display their massive wooden butcher blocks.) For the best energy, come early in the morning or late at night, especially for the 24/7 tavernas.

❷ Fruit and Veg

Across Athinas from the main hall, **produce sellers** set up here every day. The vegetables are lovely to admire, as well as an indicator of what's in peak season – and hence, what to order at restaurants. Surrounding it all are dealers in olives and cheeses, as well as some deeply absorbing junk shops.

❸ Regional Specialities

For a more structured shopping experience, head straight to the expansive **Pantopoleion** (☎210 323 4612; www.atenco.gr; Sofokleous 1, Omonia; ⏰8am-7pm), stocked with traditional products from all over Greece: Santorini capers, Cretan rusks, jars of goodies for edible souvenirs, and Greek wines and spirits.

❹ Spice Shops

Along the streets around the market, burlap bags overflow with chillies, dried rosebuds and candied ginger. Wander and enjoy the aromas emanating from shops like **Bahar** (☎210 321 7225; www.bahar.gr; Evripidou 31, Omonia; ⏰7am-3pm Mon-Thu & Sat, to 6pm Fri). Farther down Evripidou, deli **Miran** (☎210 321 7187; www.miran.gr; Evripidou 45, Psyrri) puts the spices to use on its famous *pastourma* (cured beef).

❺ Quirky Taverna

There's no signage at **Diporto Agoras** (☎210 321 1463; cnr Theatrou & Sokratous; plates €5-7; ⏰7am-7pm Mon-Sat, closed 1-20 Aug), one of the dining gems of Athens. Double doors lead to a rustic cellar, where there's also no menu. The speciality is *revythia* (chickpeas), followed by grilled fish and washed down with wine from giant barrels. Often-erratic service is part of the appeal.

❻ Contemporary Art

After lunch, see what's new at two good galleries: **A.antonopoulou. art** (☎210 321 4994; www.aaart.gr; Aristofanous 20, 4th fl, Psyrri; ⏰2-8pm Wed-Fri, noon-4pm Sat) and, just around the corner, **Alibi** (☎6938234240; Sarri 12, Psyrri; ⏰noon-5pm Tue & Sun, 4-8.30pm Wed-Fri, noon-8.30pm Sat). Excellent street art on these blocks too.

Explore
Syntagma & Plaka

Syntagma, the heart of modern Athens, is all business by day, but after the shops close scores of small bars open. Just a short walk away is the heart of old Athens, Plaka, where narrow streets wind by neoclassical mansions and pretty tavernas. It's ground zero for Athens tourism, but still home to lifelong residents.

Start with the changing of the guard (p82) in front of Parliament and a stroll through the National Gardens (p82), and add on any number of intriguing small museums, such as the Jewish Museum (p82) and the Museum of Greek Popular Instruments (p83). (Plan to visit these in the morning, as many close by early afternoon.) After lunch at Evgenia (p88), say, spend the afternoon picking up souvenirs: beauty products at Korres (p93), crafts at Flâneur (p93) and more. Then wander uphill, following any enticing set of stairs. Melina (p91) is great for a coffee break. For dinner, start at casual Kalderimi (p86) then head around the corner to The Clumsies (p90) and other neighbourhood bars. Be sure to swing by Plateia Syntagmatos again, to see a nice cross-section of Athens gathered here.

Getting There & Around

Ⓜ Syntagma station (blue and red lines) sits at the heart of the city, at Plateia Syntagmatos and a short walk from Plaka.

Ⓜ Monastiraki (blue and green lines) and Akropoli (red line) are also walking distance to Plaka.

Neighbourhood Map on p80

Yiasemi cafe (p89) on Mnisikleous stairs, Plaka T.SLACK/SHUTTERSTOCK ©

Walking Tour 🥾

Quiet Corners of Plaka & Syntagma

Move away from the touristy lowlands of Plaka for a glimpse of old Athens – virtually car-free – in narrow lanes winding up the northeastern side of the Acropolis hill, and in the maze of the Anafiotika quarter. Even modern Syntagma shows traces of history when you know where to look.

Walk Facts
Start Mnisikleous, Plaka
Finish Stadiou, Syntagma
Length 2.4km; two hours

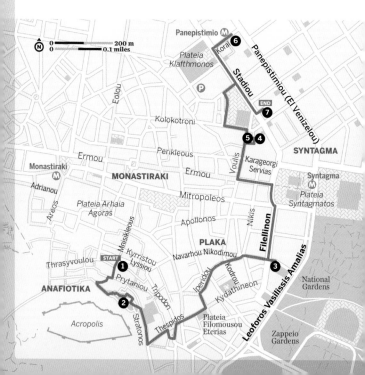

❶ Scenic Staircase

Start at perhaps the most photogenic street in Plaka, Mniskleous, where cafes line a long staircase. Neighbourhood residents favour **Yiasemi** (p89) for its tempting cakes. Pull up a pillow and perch on the stairs – you're part of the postcard now.

❷ An Island in the City

Further uphill, the tiny **Anafiotika** (p83) area grew in the mid-1800s, when builders from Anafi mimicked their home-island architecture, all whitewash and geraniums. Look for Theorias, a very small street up from Pritaniou. Zigzagging back down the southeast side via Stratonos, you'll also pass a surprise **olive grove/local park**.

❸ Byzantine Church

The 1031 **Church of Sotira Lykodimou** (p84) is the largest medieval structure in Athens. It has served as the Russian Orthodox Church since 1847.

❹ Old-School Lunch

Downtown's shopping arcades yield treasures like **Kentrikon** (☎210 323 2482; http://estiatorio-kentrikon.gr; Kolokotroni 3, Syntagma; mains €12-19; ⏰noon-8pm Mon-Sat; Ⓜ Syntagma), a white-tablecloth, wood-panelled restaurant seemingly untouched by time, serving Greek home-style standards to business lunchers and the senior set. Prefer new school? Grab premium coffee at tiny **Kaya** (Voulis 7, Syntagma; ⏰7am-6pm Mon-Fri, 8am-3pm Sat; Ⓜ Syntagma), next door.

❺ Chocolate Fix

For a dessert, stop at **Aristokratikon** (☎210 322 0546; www.aristokratikon.com; Voulis 7, Syntagma; ⏰8am-9pm Mon-Fri, to 4pm Sat; Ⓜ Syntagma), which has been making fine chocolates since 1928. One speciality: candied citrus peel in dark chocolate. It's part of the small nuts-and-sweets district centred on Karageorgi Servias.

❻ History Underground

Tucked amid chain coffee bars, the entrance to the basement of **Koraï 4** (Memorial Site 1941–44; ☎210 324 3581; www.korai4.gr; Koraï 4, Panepistimio; admission free; ⏰9am-2pm Tue-Sun; Ⓜ Panepistimio) is easy to miss. During German occupation in WWII the Gestapo used these rooms as holding cells, and the walls are scratched and sketched with messages from prisoners.

❼ Time Machine Bar

Another shopping-arcade secret: **Galaxy Bar** (☎210 322 7733; Stadiou 10, Syntagma; ⏰1pm-late Mon-Sat; Ⓜ Syntagma), a lovely vintage place that, when it opened in the 1970s, was considered truly modern because it had a proper European-style stand-up bar. Its current style can be summarised in the framed photos of the Rat Pack and Franz Kafka.

Syntagma & Plaka

A **B** **C** **D**

1

Pallados

Vyssis

Miltiadou

Nikiou

Church of
Agi Theodori

17

31

Praxitelous

Plateia
Karytsi

Karytsi

2

Miaouli

Athinas

Avramiotou

Karori

Plateia
Agia
Irini

Skouze

Limbona

Klitiou

25

Romvis

Kolokotroni

28

Thiseos

27

Lekka

4

Athinaidos

Perikleous

Ermou

Monastiraki

Ermou

Evangelistrias

Diomias

3

Monastiraki

Pandrosou

Eolou

Plateia
Kapnikareas

Mitropoleos

Fokionos

29

Petraki

Plateia
Mitropoleos

Ipatas

Patron

Pendelis

4

Areos

Dexippou

Museum of
Greek Popular
Instruments

Adrianou

Pelopida 5

Oldest
House in
Athens

14

39

42

Benizelou
Paleologou

Agias Filotheis

Thoukididou

Apollonos

30

Ipitou

PLAKA

23

Navarhou Nikodimou

Museum of
Greek
Folk Art at
22 Panos

11

12

Bath House
of the Winds

26

Mnisikleous

Kyrristou

Lyssiou

33

Erehtheos

37

Flessa

38

Scholiou

Adrianou

Iperidou

5

Theorias

7

Kanellopoulos
Museum

Prytaniou

Anafiotika 6

ANAFIOTIKA

Al Hammam
Baths

16

Tripodon

Kekropos

13

Centre of
Folk Art &
Tradition

21

44

35

32

19

Kydathineon

Plateia
Filomousou
Eterias

Church
of Agia
Ekaterin

6

For reviews see	
⊙ Sights	p82
⊗ Eating	p86
⊗ Drinking	p89
⊕ Entertainment	p91
⊕ Shopping	p93

Stratonos

Rangava

43

10

36

A **B** **C** **D**

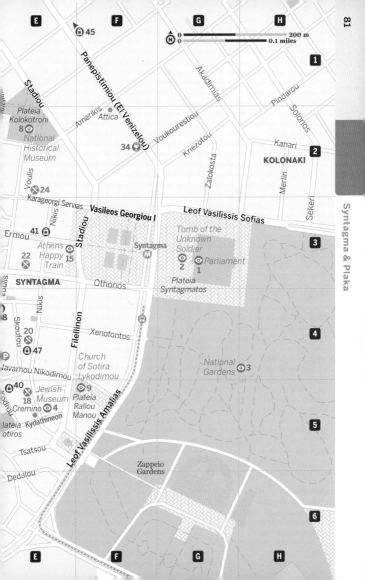

E · F · G · H

🔒 45

N 0 ――――― 200 m
   0 ――――― 0.1 miles

Panepistimiou (El Venizelou)

Akadimias

Pindarou

Solonos

Stadiou

Plateia
Kolokotroni
8 ⊗

National
Historical
Museum

Amerikis

Attica

Voukourestiou

Kriezotou

Zalokosta

Kanari

KOLONAKI

Merlin

Sekeri

34 ⊗

Voulis

⊗ 24

Karageorgi Servias

Nikis

Vasileos Georgiou I

Leof Vasilissis Sofias

Tomb of the
Unknown
Soldier
2 ⊚   ⊚ Parliament
          1

Ermou

41 🔒

Athens
Happy
Train

22 ⊗   15 ⊚

SYNTAGMA

Stadiou

Syntagma Ⓜ

Othonos

Plateia
Syntagmatos

Nikis

8

Skoutou

20 ⊗

🔒 47

Javarhou Nikodimou

Filellinon

Xenofontos

Church
of Sotira
Lykodimou

National
Gardens ⊚ 3

🔒 40

18

Cremino ⊚ 4

lateia
otiros

Jewish
Museum
⊚ 9

Plateia
Rallou
Manou

Leof Vasilissis Amalias

Kydathineon

Tsatsou

Dedalou

Zappeio
Gardens

E · F · G · H

Sights

Parliament

HISTORIC BUILDING

1 MAP P80, G3

Built between 1836 and 1842 by Bavarian architect Friedrich von Gärtner, Greece's Parliament was originally the royal palace. From its balcony, the *syntagma* (constitution) was declared on 3 September 1843, and in 1935 the palace became the seat of parliament. For history and politics geeks, the building is open by guided tour a few months of the year; book at least five days ahead. (www.hellenicparliament.gr; Plateia Syntagmatos, Syntagma; admission free; ⏱tours 3pm Mon & Fri Jun, Jul & Sep; MSyntagma)

Tomb of the Unknown Soldier

MONUMENT

2 MAP P80, G3

In front of the parliament building (p82), the traditionally costumed *evzones* (presidential guards) stand by the tomb and change every hour on the hour. On Sunday at 11am, a whole platoon marches down Vasilissis Sofias to the tomb, accompanied by a band. The *evzones* uniform of the *fustanella* (white skirt) and pom-pom shoes is based on the attire worn by the *klephts,* the mountain fighters of the War of Independence. (Plateia Syntagmatos, Syntagma; admission free; MSyntagma)

National Gardens

GARDENS

3 MAP P80, H4

The former royal gardens, designed by Queen Amalia in 1938, are a pleasantly unkempt park that makes a welcome shady refuge from summer heat and traffic. Tucked among the trees are a cafe, a playground, turtle and duck ponds, and a tiny (if slightly dispiriting) zoo. The main entrance is on Leoforos Vasilissis Sofias, south of parliament; you can also enter from Irodou Attikou to the east, or from the adjacent Zappeio Gardens (p121) to the south. (admission free; ⏱7am-dusk; MSyntagma)

Jewish Museum

MUSEUM

4 MAP P80, E5

This small museum traces the history of the Jewish community in Greece – starting with the deeply rooted Romaniote community established in the 3rd century BCE, through the arrival of Sephardic Jews and beyond the Holocaust. The documents, religious art and folk objects are beautifully presented. It's worth visiting to learn the story of the bishop and the mayor of Zakynthos, the only Greek leaders who managed to save the Jewish community from Nazi round-ups. (☎210 322 5582; www.jewishmuseum.gr; Nikis 39, Plaka; adult/child €6/free; ⏱9am-2.30pm Mon-Fri, 10am-2pm Sun; MSyntagma)

Museum of Greek Popular Instruments   MUSEUM

5 ◉ MAP P80, B4

A single avid ethnomusicologist collected almost 1200 folk instruments; the best are on display in three floors of this house-turned-museum. Headphones let visitors listen to the *gaida* (Greek goatskin bagpipes) and the wood planks priests on Mt Athos use to call prayer times, among other distinctly Greek sounds. Musical performances are held in the lovely garden in summer. (☎210 325 4119; http://odysseus.culture.gr; Diogenous 1-3, Plaka; admission free; ☺10am-2pm Tue & Thu-Sun, noon-6pm Wed; Ⓜ Monastiraki)

Anafiotika   AREA

6 ◉ MAP P80, B5

Clinging to the north slope of the Acropolis, the tiny Anafiotika district is a beautiful, architecturally distinct subdistrict of Plaka. In the mid-1800s, King Otto hired builders from Anafi to build a new palace. In their homes here, they mimicked their island architecture, all whitewashed cubes, bedecked with bougainvillea and geraniums. The area now is a clutch of about 40 homes, linked by footpaths just wide enough for people and donkeys. (Stratonos, Plaka; Ⓜ Monastiraki, Akropoli)

Syntagma & Plaka Sights

Guards outside the Tomb of the Unknown Soldier

Kanellopoulos Museum
MUSEUM

7 ⊙ MAP P80, A5

A neoclassical mansion contains a family's collection that was bequeathed to the Greek state in the 1970s. There's lovely classical and Byzantine art and jewellery, and especially transfixing terracotta and bronze classical figurines. Also note the ceilings in the Byzantine wing (the icons are great too). Signage is a bit sparse, and preservation conditions aren't ideal, but as the place is often empty of other visitors, it can feel like you're touring your own eclectic collection. (☏210 321 2313; http://odysseus.culture.gr; Theorias 12, cnr Panos, Plaka; adult/child €4/2; ⊙8am-3pm Tue-Sun, reduced hours in low season; Ⓜ Monastiraki)

National Historical Museum
MUSEUM

8 ⊙ MAP P80, E2

This grand old collection of swords, ship figureheads and portraits of moustachioed generals is a bit short on signage, so it's best for people who already know something about modern Greek history and the many battles of the 19th century that built the nation, piece by piece. This includes the battle of Messolonghi, where Lord Byron fought; the museum owns the camp bed on which he died of malaria, among other effects – though they are often out on loan.

(☏210 323 7617; www.nhmuseum.gr; Stadiou 13, Syntagma; adult/child €3/free; ⊙8.30am-2.30pm Tue-Sun; Ⓜ Syntagma)

Church of Sotira Lykodimou
CHURCH

9 ⊙ MAP P80, F5

First built in the 11th century and now the Russian Orthodox Cathedral, this is the only Byzantine church with an octagonal plan. It's quite small but topped with a high dome, so the whole space, glittering with gold stars and icons, soars upward. Neoclassical icons by the famed portrait painter Nikiforos Lytras (done when he was still a student at the School of Fine Arts in the mid-1800s) add a slightly uncanny realist touch. (Fillelinon, Plateia Rallou Manou, Plaka; Ⓜ Syntagma)

Church of Agia Ekaterini
CHURCH

10 ⊙ MAP P80, D6

One of the few very old Byzantine churches that is open regularly, this one is definitely worth a peek inside to see how an 11th-century space is still in vibrant use and adorned with bright frescoes. For a time it was the property of the Monastery of St Catherine in the Sinai Peninsula, which is how it took on that saint's name. In the front yard are some Roman ruins. (Lysikratous 3, Plaka; ⊙8am-noon & varied evening hours; Ⓜ Akropoli)

Museum of Greek Folk Art at 22 Panos
MUSEUM

11 ⊙ MAP P80, A5

While the main Museum of Greek Folk Art is being rebuilt, this annexe houses the permanent collection *Men & Tools,* which is not quite as dry as it sounds. The small display, enhanced with music, is a loving tribute to Greeks' hard labour and refined skills in the preindustrial era. (www.melt.gr; Panos 22, Plaka; adult/child €2/1; ⊙8am-3pm Tue-Sun)

Bath House of the Winds
MUSEUM

12 ⊙ MAP P80, B4

One of the few remnants of Athens' Ottoman period, this 17th-century *hammam* (Turkish bath) is also the only intact public bath building in the city – though it unfortunately no longer functions as such. As a museum, though, it's quite pretty, with music, sound and a few projections conjuring its glory days as you stroll through the various rooms. (☏210 324 4340; www.melt.gr; Kyrristou 8, Monastiraki; adult/child €2/free; ⊙8am-3pm Wed-Mon; Ⓜ Monastiraki)

Centre of Folk Art & Tradition
MUSEUM

13 ⊙ MAP P80, D5

The 1920s mansion of folklorist Angeliki Hatzimichalis, who wrote more than 100 books and articles about Greek traditions, is a window into daily life of yore. Compared to the vast collection of

Anafiotika (p83)

IRAKLIS / SHUTTERSTOCK ©

The Other Evzones

Guards in traditional dress are also posted along Irodou Attikou, behind the parliament building, and it's fascinating to see them here, alone and away from tourist cameras, going through their ritual pomp – even in the dead of night.

the Benaki Museum (p100) it feels scant, but it's a pretty house and a nice dip into regional costumes, embroidery and more, along with family portraits. (☎ 210 324 3987; www.cityofathens.gr; Hatzimihali Angelikis 6, Plaka; admission free; ☉ 9am-7pm Tue-Fri, to 2pm Sat & Sun; Ⓜ Syntagma)

Oldest House in Athens   HOUSE

14 ◎ MAP P80, C4

Opened after renovations in 2017, the 17th-century Benizelos home is a typical domestic structure from that period, with dirt-floor downstairs rooms with wine and olive presses, and wood-panelled living rooms upstairs. Look for the repurposed classical columns in the gate leading to the backyard, formerly an olive grove. It's a nice free diversion, but note the limited opening hours. (Adrianou 96, Plaka; admission free; ☉ 10am-1pm Tue & Thu, 11am-4pm Sun; Ⓜ Monastiraki, Syntagma)

Athens Happy Train   TOURS

15 ◎ MAP P80, E3

This little red train-on-wheels is a bit goofy, but it's more city-friendly than a massive double-decker tour bus. Stops include the Acropolis, Monastiraki and the Panathenaic Stadium. Tours take one hour nonstop, or you can get on and off over the day. Trains leave from the top of Ermou every 30 minutes. (☎ 213 039 0888; www.athenshappytrain.com; Plateia Syntagmatos, Syntagma; adult/child €5/3; ☉ 9am-11pm Jun-Sep, to 9pm Oct-May; Ⓜ Syntagma)

Al Hammam Baths   BATHHOUSE

16 ◎ MAP P80, C5

Like the other two Turkish-style baths in Athens, this one is a bit small, but it is beautifully decorated, in marble and tile and coloured chandeliers, to conjure an old-Ottoman atmosphere. Moreover, it's set in a nice old house in Plaka, so after your steam and skin scrub, you can have tea on the terrace and admire the Acropolis. (☎ 211 012 9099; www.alhammam.gr; Tripodon 16, Plaka; 45min bath €25, bath-scrub combos from €35; ☉ 11am-10pm; Ⓜ Acropolis)

Eating

Kalderimi   TAVERNA €

17 ✕ MAP P80, C1

Look behind the **Church of Agii Theodori** (Map p80, C1) for this taverna offering Greek food at its most authentic. Everything is freshly cooked and delicious: you can't go wrong. Hand-painted tables edge a pedestrian street, providing for a feeling of peace in one of the busiest parts of the city. (It helps that it closes just before nearby bars get rolling.) (📞210 331 0049; Plateia Agion Theodoron, cnr Skouleniou, Monastiraki; mains €6-8; ⏰11am-8pm Mon-Thu, to 10pm Fri & Sat; 🛜; Ⓜ Panepistimio)

Palia Athina   TAVERNA €

18 🍴 MAP P80, E5

No muss, no fuss, no music or show: just a quiet little family-run taverna with excellent prices (especially for the area) and good food. The stews and casseroles are solid; the stuffed calamari is excellent. Also does delivery or takeaway, if you're too tired to leave the hotel room. (📞210 324 5777; Nikis 46, Syntagma; mains €6-12; ⏰noon-11pm; Ⓜ Syntagma)

Damigos   TAVERNA €

19 🍴 MAP P80, D6

A real treat in Plaka, hidden away and intimate feeling, this tradition-al place specialises in *bakaliaros*, toothsome cod fried in pillow-light batter and spiked with garlicky dip. Everything else is good too, aided by quality house wine, naturally chilled in barrels set in the bed-rock. It's been open since 1865. Look for the entrance just right of Brettos bar. (📞210 322 5084; www. mpakaliarakia.gr; Kydathineon 41, Plaka; mains €8-10; ⏰2pm-midnight; Ⓜ Akropoli)

Avocado   VEGETARIAN €

20 🍴 MAP P80, E4

This popular cafe offers a full array of vegan, gluten-free and organic treats, with an international spin. Next to an organic market, and with a tiny front patio, here you can enjoy everything from sand-wiches to quinoa with aubergine or mixed-veg coconut curry. Juices and mango lassis are all made on the spot. (📞210 323 7878; www. avocadoathens.com; Nikis 30, Plaka; mains €8-13; ⏰noon-11pm Mon-Fri, 11am-11pm Sat, noon-7pm Sun; 🛜 ✍; Ⓜ Syntagma)

Glykys   MEZEDHES €

21 🍴 MAP P80, D5

In a quiet corner of Plaka, this low-key place with a shady front yard is mostly frequented by students and locals. It has a tasty selection of mezedhes, including

Traditional Ice Cream

The lovely proprietress at **Cremino** (Map p80, E5; Nikis 50a, Plaka; scoops €2.20; ⏰11.30am-6.30pm, later in spring & summer; Ⓜ Syntagma, Akropoli) makes gelato and sorbet that's both intensely flavoured and incredibly light, using cow and buffalo milk. Flavours change daily, but look for creamy-chewy *kaïmaki*, a classic recipe with Chios mastic resin and orchid root.

Brettos bar (p91)

traditional dishes such as *briam* (oven-baked vegetable casserole) and cuttlefish in wine. (📞210 322 3925; www.glykys.gr; Angelou Geronta 2, Plaka; mezedhes €4-8; ⏰10am-1am; Ⓜ Akropoli)

Tzitzikas kai Mermigas
MEZEDHES €€

22 ❌ MAP P80, E3

Greek merchandise lines the walls of this cheery, modern place that sits smack in the middle of central Athens. It serves a tasty range of delicious and creative dishes, such as honey-drizzled, bacon-wrapped Naxos cheese, to a bustling crowd of locals and tourists. (📞210 324

7607; www.tzitzikasmermigas.gr; Mitropoleos 12-14, Syntagma; mezedhes €6-12; ⏰noon-11pm; Ⓜ Syntagma)

Evgenia
TAVERNA €€

23 ❌ MAP P80, D4

For great traditional fare, it's hard to beat this inconspicuous, no-frills taverna on the periphery of Plaka, with a few tables on the footpath. There's a standard menu but it's best to choose from the daily specials, which can include fresh seafood such as prawn saganaki. (Paradosiako; 📞210 321 4121; Voulis 44a, Plaka; mains €7-13; ⏰lunch & dinner; 📶; Ⓜ Syntagma)

Metropolis

SANDWICHES €

24 MAP P80, E2

When you want a quick pick-me-up that's not souvlaki, head for this tiny sandwich shop that makes delicious, sophisticated sandwiches. The open-face house-marinated salmon sandwich and the freshly squeezed juice are tops. (☑ 210 322 2122; Voulis 9-11, Syntagma; sandwiches €3.50-6; ⏰ 8am-6.30pm Mon & Wed, to 9pm Tue, Thu & Fri, 10am-6pm Sat; Ⓜ Syntagma)

Drinking

Baba Au Rum

COCKTAIL BAR

25 🍷 MAP P80, C2

As the name implies, the focus here is on rum drinks, with an excellent selection of rarer Caribbean rums and a whole range of cocktails, from classic tiki drinks to new inventions. This is just one of a handful of good little bars in this strip. (☑ 211 710 9140; www.babaaurum.com; Klitiou 6, Monastiraki; ⏰ 7pm-3am Sun-Fri, 1pm-4am Sat; Ⓜ Syntagma, Monastiraki)

Yiasemi

CAFE

26 🍷 MAP P80, B5

Proof that Plaka is still very much a Greek neighbourhood, despite the tourists, this cafe attracts a good mix of young Athenians, who set up for hours in the big armchairs

Stoa Life

Take any chance you get to duck into the stoas (shopping arcades) that cut through large buildings around Syntagma. Away from the street, where rent is cheaper, you might find old-man *ouzeries* (places serving ouzo and snacks), single-purpose stores, a jewel-box cocktail bar, even an occasional pop-up DJ party. Stairs down to basement level are often fruitful too.

or out on the scenic steps. It's better by day (especially for the great veg breakfast buffet) and on weeknights, when it's not overwhelmed by the scene at nearby restaurants. (☑ 213 041 7937; www.yiasemi.gr; Mnisikleous 23, Plaka; ⏰ 10am-3am; Ⓜ Monastiraki)

Ippo

BAR

27 🍷 MAP P80, D2

This great little place caters to the slightly more mature bar-crawler, with pinball, David Bowie and old soul on the sound system, and better-than-average bar snacks. The bathrooms are a whole other world. (☑ 213 005 4715; Thiseos 11; ⏰ 7.30pm-2am Sun-Thu, to 4am Fri & Sat; Ⓜ Syntagma)

Barley Cargo

BAR

28 ⊕ MAP P80, D2

If you think Greek beer begins and ends with Alpha, head here to learn more. The big open-front bar stocks the products of many Greek microbreweries, as well as more than 100 international beers. Live music is a bonus. (☎210 323 0445; Kolokotroni 6, Syntagma; ⏱11am-3am, from 5pm Sun; Ⓜ Syntagma)

Heteroclito

WINE BAR

29 ⊕ MAP P80, D3

This relaxed wine bar, all mismatched vintage furniture, showcases the best of Greek vintages, paired with Greek cheeses and cold cuts. It periodically organises tasting events. The name is Greek for 'maverick'. (☎210 323 9406; www.heteroclito.gr; Fokionos 2, Monastiraki; ⏱12.30pm-midnight Mon-Thu, to 1.30am Fri & Sat, 6pm-midnight Sun; Ⓜ Monastiraki)

Kiki de Grece

WINE BAR

30 ⊕ MAP P80, D4

Man Ray's muse, Kiki de Montparnasse, declared that in hard times, all she needed was bread, an onion and a bottle of red wine. This pedestrian-street bar also takes her as its muse, and offers plenty more than a bottle of red. There's a huge range from Greece's vintners, paired with seasonal dishes from various regions in Greece. (☎210 321 1279; www.facebook.com/kikide grece; Ipitou 4; ⏱noon-1am, to 2am Sat; Ⓜ Syntagma)

Clumsies

BAR

31 ⊕ MAP P80, C1

Look for the red neon in the hallway of this unsigned bar that fills your coffee and creative cocktail needs. Founded by three award-winning bartenders, it is very serious about its drinks, but the atmosphere is definitely fun, and full of slick, handsome types on the weekends. (☎210 323 2682; www.theclumsies.gr; Praxitelous 30, Syntagma; ⏱10am-2am Sun-Thu, to 4am Fri & Sat; Ⓜ Syntagma)

Cocktails at a bar

DAVID TADEVOSIAN/SHUTTERSTOCK ©

Brettos   BAR

32 🍸 MAP P80, D6

Plaka is short on bars in general, but Brettos, both a bar and a distillery, makes up for it. It's small, delightfully old and glowing with walls of coloured bottles and huge barrels. Sample its home brands of wine, ouzo, brandy and other spirits. (📞 210 323 2110; www.brettos plaka.com; Kydathineon 41, Plaka; ⏰ 10am-3am; Ⓜ Akropoli)

Melina   CAFE

33 🍸 MAP P80, C5

A tribute to the great Mercouri, this cafe-bar is decorated with portraits of the actress and politician who lobbied for the repatriation of the missing Parthenon marbles. Mercouri's most famous for the film *Never on Sunday,* but in fact that's a great day to come, when it's very busy and prime outdoor seats offer a view of the Plaka parade. (Lyssiou 22, Plaka; ⏰ 9am-2am; Ⓜ Akropoli, Monastiraki)

Zonar's   CAFE

34 🍸 MAP P80, F2

It's worth the steep price of a coffee or cocktail (€15) just to lounge in the sumptuous interior of this famous cafe, all velvet and brass and walnut panelling. In the 1950s and 1960s, it claimed patrons such as Simone de Beauvoir and Sophia Loren, and, following a 2016 renovation, it still hosts a distinctly elegant scene. (📞 210 325 1430; www.zonarsathens.gr;

Party Smart

● Syntagma's main bar zones are Plateia Karytsi and along Kolokotroni.

● Pace yourself. Public drunkenness is frowned on, and makes you an easy target for pickpockets or phone-grabbers.

● If you like electronic dance music, visit tiny record shop **Kasseta** (Sofokleous 5; ⏰ 1-10pm Tue, noon-5pm Wed, 1-9pm Thu & Fri, noon-5pm Sat) for flyers and info on parties.

Voukourestiou 9; ⏰ 9am-3am, to 4am Fri & Sat; Ⓜ Syntagma)

Entertainment

Cine Paris   CINEMA

35 ⭐ MAP P80, D5

The Paris was established in the 1920s, and it's still a magical place to see a movie, on a rooftop in Plaka with great views of the Acropolis from some seats. (📞 210 322 0721; www.cineparis.gr; Kydathineon 22, Plaka; ⏰ May-Oct; Ⓜ Syntagma)

Perivoli tou Ouranou   TRADITIONAL MUSIC

36 ⭐ MAP P80, D6

A favourite Plaka music haunt with dinner (mains €18 to €29). (📞 210 323 5517; www.perivolitouranou.gr; Lysikratous 19, Plaka; ⏰ 9pm-late Fri & Sat, noon-6pm Sun Oct-Jun; Ⓜ Akropoli)

Athens in Double Crisis

In Athens' busy streets and lively cafes you may not immediately see *i krisi* – the financial crisis that Greeks have been labouring under since 2010. Conditions here are better than in rural areas, but tax hikes and drastic pension cuts – imposed as terms of a series of bailout loans from the EU and the International Monetary Foundation – have touched everyone and widened Greece's already stark economic divide.

Homelessness, suicide, drug use and once-rare burglary and violent crime have risen. Highly educated young Greeks face a youth unemployment rate of around 45%, which has prompted many to flee for jobs in other countries.

The most chaotic point may have been the near-collapse of banks in 2015, and the baffling about-face of anti-austerity prime minister Alexis Tsipras, who signed another bailout deal just three days after the public voted a resounding 'no' in a referendum. Mass strikes and violent clashes with the police followed. Around the same time, refugees fleeing conflict and persecution in Syria, Iraq, Afghanistan, Eritrea and various countries in West Africa began arriving in Greece by the thousands every day. For a time, the port of Piraeus and Plateia Viktoria were informal encampments.

Athens city government has embraced the influx, stating that immigration is an opportunity for growth. And indeed, immigration, which first started in earnest in the 1990s, has reinvigorated neighbourhoods: Psyrri has a strip of Bangladeshi and Pakistani shops, and Metaxourgio bursts with Chinese wholesalers. Newer arrivals have enlivened the squat scene in Exarhia as well as the Viktoria neighbourhood. Further north, the blocks around Plateia Amerikis have attracted immigrants from West Africa and Eritrea.

As for the economic picture, August 2018 marked the end of the last bailout period, and, theoretically, the point at which the economy may again begin to expand. So far, the economic indicators are showing faint promise. But it will be years before the despair and anxiety fully lifts.

Stamatopoulos TRADITIONAL MUSIC

37 MAP P80, C5

This Plaka restaurant, established in 1882, has live music nightly and Sunday afternoons. It is now so legendary that it can feel a bit like a film set. The food (mains €8 to €13) is plain but good, and the crowd, in two garden-like levels outside or cosy in the mural-covered dining room, gets more local as the night wears on. (📞210 322 8722; www.stamatopoulostavern.gr; Lyssiou 26, Plaka; ⏰7pm-2am Mon-Sat, 11am-2am Sun; Ⓜ Monastiraki)

Shopping

Flâneur   DESIGN

38 🅰 MAP P80, C5

This cute shop has a tightly curated collection of souvenirs and travel gear. Get your hand-stamped 'φλανέρ' (that's 'flâneur' spelled in Greek) notebooks and your feta-tin patches and pins here. Even stocks vinyl by Greek indie bands. (📞210 322 6900; Adrianou 110, cnr Flessa, Plaka; ⏰11am-8pm; Ⓜ Syntagma, Monastiraki)

Forget Me Not   GIFTS & SOUVENIRS

39 🅰 MAP P80, C4

This impeccable small store (well, two shops, one upstairs and one down around the corner) stocks supercool gear, from fashion to housewares and gifts, all by con-temporary Greek designers. Great for gift shopping – who doesn't want a set of cheerful 'evil eye' coasters or some Hermes-winged beach sandals? (📞210 325 3740; www.forgetmenotathens.gr; Adrianou 100, Plaka; ⏰10am-10pm May-Sep, to 8pm Oct-Apr; Ⓜ Syntagma, Monas-tiraki)

Amorgos   ARTS & CRAFTS

40 🅰 MAP P80, E5

Charming store crammed with wooden toys, *karagiozi* (shadow

puppets), ceramics, embroidery and other Greek folk art, as well as carved wooden furniture made by the owner. (📞210 324 3836; www.amorgosart.gr; Kodrou 3, Plaka; ⏰11am-8pm Mon-Fri, to 7pm Sat; Ⓜ Syntagma)

Korres   COSMETICS

41 🅰 MAP P80, E3

Many pharmacies stock some of this popular line of natural beauty products, but you can get the full range at the company's original location, where it grew out of a homeopathic pharmacy. (📞210 321 0054; www.korres.com; Ermou 4, Syntagma; ⏰9am-9pm Mon-Fri, to 8pm Sat; Ⓜ Syntagma)

Greek pottery

Best Shopping Streets

Adrianou Lined with souvenir shops – many generic, but an increasing number stocking interesting new designs. Shops here are generally open late.

Ermou Athens' first modern street of shops, and now mostly chains, but nice to stroll because it's car-free. It's named for Hermes, god of trade; nearly every Greek town has its own Ermou St.

Alexis Papachatzis   JEWELLERY

42 🔒 MAP P80, C4

This charming jewellery store is a delight before you even enter: turn the handle on the window display and watch as gears and pulleys animate the scene. Papachatzis' designs have a storybook quality, in small figures, clouds and animals rendered in sterling silver and enamel. (📞210 325 4064; www.alexisp.gr; Erehtheos 6; ⏱10am-4pm Mon, Wed & Fri, 10am-7pm Tue, Thu & Sat; Ⓜ Monastiraki, Syntagma)

Fine Wine   WINE

43 🔒 MAP P80, D6

In the winding streets of Plaka the finest wines can be found in this small terracotta-hued building that's a bit worn around the edges. It's a welcoming destination for the curious and for local wine lovers who come to browse the rows of vintage Greek wines lining the centuries-old stone walls. (📞210 323 0350; www.finewine.gr; Lysikratous 3, Plaka; ⏱noon-9pm; Ⓜ Akropoli)

Ioanna Kourbela   FASHION & ACCESSORIES

44 🔒 MAP P80, D5

Classic, cool fashion by a Greek designer with a preference for natural fibres. Think elegantly draped cottons and silks in natural, warm tones, and slouchy casual wear for the street. Her men's collection and couture boutiques are just around the corner, on Iperidou. (📞210 322 4591; www.ioanna kourbela.com; Adrianou 109, Plaka; ⏱10am-9pm Mon-Sat, 11am-9pm Sun; Ⓜ Syntagma)

Xylouris   MUSIC

45 🔒 MAP P80, F1

Set in an arcade with several other music shops, this treasure trove is run by the family of legendary Cretan composer Nikos Xylouris. They can guide you through the comprehensive range of Greek music, as well as a new bouzouki purchase. Also has a branch at the Museum of Greek Popular Instruments (p83). (📞210 322 2711; http://xilouris.gr; Stoa Pesmatzoglou, Panepistimiou 39, Panepistimio; ⏱9am-4pm Mon, Wed & Sat, to 8pm Tue, Thu & Fri; Ⓜ Panepistimio)

Cafes in Plaka

Actipis JEWELLERY

46 🔒 MAP P80, D2

Spiros Actipis designs elegant jewellery using smooth pebbles, gleaming silver and raw leather. The shop closes in summer, as Spiros decamps to Mykonos. (📞210 323 6907; www.actipis.com; Lekka 20, Syntagma; ⏰11.30am-8pm Mon-Fri, to 5pm Sat Nov-Apr; Ⓜ Syntagma)

Aidini ARTS & CRAFTS

47 🔒 MAP P80, E4

Artisan Errikos Aidini's unique metal creations are made in his workshop at the back of this charming store, including small mirrors, candlesticks, lamps, aeroplanes and his signature bronze boats. (📞210 323 4591; Nikis 32, Syntagma; ⏰10am-3pm Mon, Wed & Sat, to 9pm Tue, Thu & Fri, to 3pm Sat; Ⓜ Syntagma)

Anavasi MAPS, BOOKS

48 🔒 MAP P80, E4

Great travel bookshop with an extensive range of Greece maps and walking and activity guides. (📞210 321 8104; www.anavasi.gr; Voulis 32, cnr Apollonos, Syntagma; ⏰9.30am-5.30pm Mon & Wed, to 8.30pm Tue, Thu & Fri, 10am-4.30pm Sat; Ⓜ Syntagma)

Walking Tour 🚶

Central Athens Meander

Boisterous, monument-packed central Athens is best explored on foot. The historic centre, as well as the main archaeological sites, major landmarks, museums and attractions, are close to one another. The main civic hub of Athens, Plateia Syntagmatos, merges into the historic Plaka and Monastiraki neighbourhoods, which mesh one into the next, and make for a super stroll in which to soak up a bit of city-centre life.

Walk Facts

Start Plateia Syntagmatos

End Monastiraki Flea Market

Length 2.5km; three hours

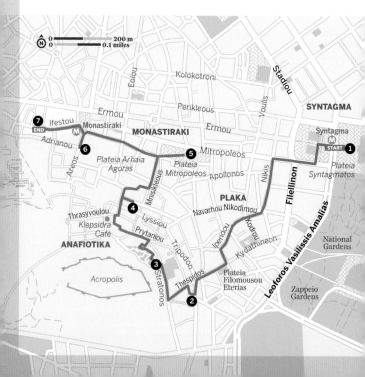

❶ Plateia Syntagmatos

This square, named for the *syntagma* (constitution) granted on 3 September 1843, is considered the centre of Athens. Time your visit with the changing of the guard at the **Tomb of the Unknown Soldier** (p82). North of the metro entrance, look for a section of the ancient cemetery and the Peisistratos aqueduct.

❷ Lysikrates Monument

Built in 334 BCE, this carved **marble pedestal** (cnr Sellei & Lysikratous, Plaka; admission free; Ⓜ Akropoli, Syntagma) was the base for a bronze tripod trophy, awarded to winners of a dramatic contest. In ancient times, this street, Tripodon, was lined with such monuments, all the way to the Theatre of Dionysos at the foot of the Acropolis.

❸ Anafiotika Quarter

On Stratonos, which skirts the Acropolis, rises the **Church of St George of the Rock**, which marks the entry to **Anafiotika** (p83), an especially picturesque corner of Plaka.

❹ Turkish Baths

Duck into the **Bath House of the Winds** (p85), a pretty late-Ottoman-era *hammam* restored as a museum. Around the corner, the gift shop of the **Museum of Greek Popular Instruments** (p83) is built atop the ruins of another set of baths.

❺ Plateia Mitropoleos

Jaunt north to **Plateia Mitropoleos**, where you'll find **Athens Cathedral** (p63) and its smaller, more historically significant neighbour, 12th-century Church of Agios Eleftherios (known as the **Little Metropolis**). Don't feel shy about using the churches as Greeks do: drop a few small coins in the slot for a beeswax candle, light it from the others and make a wish.

❻ Hadrian's Library

Pandrosou, a relic of the old Turkish bazaar, is full of souvenir shops and leads to **Hadrian's Library** (p65), once the most lavish public building in the city, erected by the eponymous Roman emperor around CE 132.

❼ Monastiraki Flea Market

Cut through the main square at Monastiraki, which teems with street vendors, and head down Ifestou to the antiques dealers clustered around Plateia Avyssinias, known as the **Monastiraki Flea Market** (p59).

✕ Take a Break

Midway along the route, on the western edge of Plaka, **Klepsidra** (☎ 210 321 2493; Klepsydras & Thrasyvoulou, Plaka; ⊙ 9am-1am; Ⓜ Monastiraki) is a delightfully quiet cafe that's popular with locals before and after work.

Explore ◈

Kolonaki

Kolonaki is an adjective as much as a district: chic, stylish, elite. The area, which stretches from near Syntagma to the slopes of Lykavittos Hill, is where old money mixes with the nouveau riche. It's home to several excellent museums, and the cool, tree-shaded streets make a lovely retreat after sun-blasted ruins. Come here to sample Athens' good life, and maybe buy some shoes.

Given the size of the Benaki Museum of Greek Culture (p100) and the Byzantine & Christian Museum (p106), it's hard to visit both in a single day. The Museum of Cycladic Art (p106) is smaller, and a manageable add-on to the two biggies.

*Whichever you visit, it's nice to fuel up with coffee on Plateia Kolonakiou, or lunch at a chic Skoufa cafe like Nice N' Easy (p109). Afterward, shoppers can pop in to Kolonaki's many boutiques. And as in most Athens neighbourhoods, there's a hill to climb. **Lykavittos** ('Hill of Wolves', from when the area was a bit wilder) is taller than most, but it offers a funicular as a shortcut. The view at night over the whole glittering cityscape is impressive, and there's a bar-cafe up here to enjoy.*

Getting There & Around

Ⓜ Evangelismos (blue line) for the eastern extents of Kolonaki.

Ⓜ Syntagma (blue and red lines) for the western edge.

Neighbourhood Map on p104

View over Athens from Lykavittos Hill (p103)
ANDREA PUCCI/GETTY IMAGES ©

Top Experience 📷

Immerse Yourself at the Benaki Museum of Greek Culture

Antonis Benakis was a politician's son born in Alexandria, Egypt, in the late 19th century. After decades of collecting, in 1930 he turned the family's house into a museum. Now three storeys and many rooms larger, the museum presents all facets of Greek culture through the ages, with just the right amount of everything, and all of it beautiful.

◉ MAP P104, C5

www.benaki.gr

Koumbari 1, cnr Leoforos Vasilissis Sofias, Kolonaki

adult/student/child €9/7/fre

🕑 9am-5pm Wed & Fri, to midnight Thu & Sat, to 4pm Sun

Ⓜ Syntagma, Evangelism

Ground Floor

Flint Flakes

In room 1, these shards of flint chipped into tool shapes date from 50,000–40,000 BCE, in the Middle Paleolithic period – maybe the oldest human-made thing you'll ever see.

Cretan School Painters

In the last room on the ground floor, gallery 12, are masterpieces from Venetian-held Crete (15th–16th centuries). These include works by Domenikos Theotokopoulos (later known as El Greco, 1541–1614), and several by Theodoros Poulakis (1622–1692). The Cretan School developed techniques still used in icons today: sharp outlines, a geometric depiction of fabrics, and subtly highlighted skin tones.

First Floor

Kozani Rooms

The rooms dedicated to the wealth of 18th- and 19th-century Epiros, themselves quite dazzling, lead into two reception halls that have been re-located from mansions in neighbouring Kozani, Macedonia. They are confections of carved and painted wood and stained glass.

Folk Costumes

Also on the 1st floor is room upon room of the finest and most intricately fashioned traditional clothing, showing the diversity of the islands and the various regions of the mainland, including the Peloponnese, Epiros, Macedonia and Thrace. The spacious displays are interspersed with other priceless objects, such as carved marble door frames and jewel-encrusted Ottoman crowns.

★ Top Tips

o Thursday is a prime day to visit: free admission and the museum is open till midnight.

o A €25 pass is valid for one visit to each of the Benaki museums – including the modern/contemporary 138 Pireos St (p163) and the Museum of Islamic Art, (p163) plus six other smaller sites – over three months.

✖ Take a Break

The Benaki's cafe (p109) is renowned for great food in an open dining room, stretching out onto a terrace overlooking the national gardens and the Acropolis.

Otherwise, pop over to one of Plateia Kolonakiou's cafes like Da Capo (p111).

Walking Tour 🥾

People-Watching in Kolonaki

If you're familiar with any Greek celebrities, you'll have a chance of spotting them in Kolonaki, a wealthy neighbourhood favoured by actors, politicians and journalists who prefer city life to the suburbs. Even if you don't recognise anyone, you can still admire a parade of aristocrats and fashionistas, all focused on the key Kolonaki goals: looking good and feeling good..

Walk Facts

Start Skoufa at Lykavittou

Finish Dinokratous near Plateia Dexameni

Length 1.8km; two hours

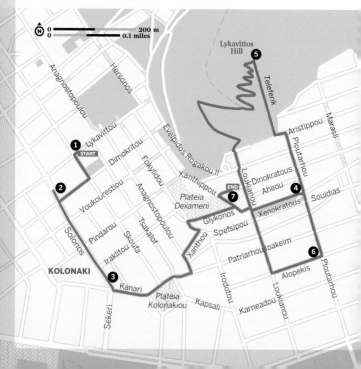

❶ Coffee Klatch

The extended people-watching session – with coffee on the side – is a Kolonaki pastime. Its historical roots are at **Filion** (☏210 361 2850; www.filioncafe.com; Skoufa 34, Kolonaki; ⏱7am-12.30am; 🛜; Ⓜ Syntagma), where, to hear some tell it, decades of political schemes have been hatched. Now it's where the neighbourhood's old guard reads the day's paper.

❷ House Beautiful

Get an idea of how Kolonaki scenesters decorate their homes at **Graffito** (☏210 360 8936; www.graffito.gr; Solonos 34, Kolonaki; ⏱9am-5pm Mon & Wed, to 9pm Tue, Thu & Fri, 10am-6pm Sat; Ⓜ Panepistimio, Syntagma), a chic homewares shop that also happens to have a cafe specialising in raw vegan desserts.

❸ Spa Day

Learn more secrets of the beautiful people at **Apivita** (☏210 364 0560; www.apivita.com; Solonos 6, Kolonaki; ⏱10am-9pm Tue, Thu & Fri, to 5pm Mon, Wed & Sat, spa closed Mon & Sun; Ⓜ Syntagma), the boutique for the Greek brand's bee-based cosmetics and other products. A facial at the upstairs spa is a treat.

❹ Traditional Taverna

Filippou (☏210 721 6390; www.filippou.gr; Xenokratous 19, Kolonaki; mains €8-12; ⏱12.30-5pm & 7pm-midnight Mon-Fri, 1-5pm Sat; Ⓜ Evangelismos) is always packed with locals enjoying the renowned home-style fare that this classic taverna has been dishing out since 1923. White-linen-covered tables spill into the courtyard, but book ahead to ensure you get one.

❺ Lykavittos Hill

From the top of Loukianou, a path leads up Kolonaki's hill for fine panoramas of the city and the Attic basin. Alternatively, take the **funicular** (Teleferik; ☏210 721 0701; return/1-way €7.50/5; ⏱every 30min 9am-3am) from the top of Ploutarhou. Perched on the summit is the little white **Chapel of Agios Giorgios** (Lykavittos Hill, Kolonaki; Ⓜ Evangelismos), floodlit like a beacon over the city at night. If you're lucky you'll get there when a wedding is happening.

❻ Streetside Dinner

At a pavement table at modern taverna **Oikeio** (p108) you get the best of both worlds: excellent, affordable home-style cooking and a view on street life, especially as the jet set is heading out and about. Book ahead for dinner, as it always fills up.

❼ Intimate Nightcap

Retreat to Kolonaki's upper reaches at the cosy **Jazz in Jazz** (p110), perfect for a last glass of wine or whisky. Everyone looks gorgeous in the glow of candles glinting off the brass instruments that decorate the walls.

A

B

C

D

1

Mavromihali

Ippokratous

Navarinou

Asklipiou

Merlie Octaviou

Prassa G

Doxapatri

Sarandapihou

Dafnomili

Leontos Sgourou

2

Solonos

Kaplanon

Masalias

Delfon

Didotou

Sina

Statha G

Dimaki P

Anagnostopoulou

Skoufa

Itis

Hersonos

Evelpidos Rogakou II

University
of Athens

Mantzarou

Skoufa

✕12

Lykavittou

CAN
◉6

3

17 🚇

Omirou

Solonos

19 🚇

20 🚇

Lykavittou

Dimokritou

28 🔒

13✕

Voukourestiou

Tsakalof

Fokylidou

Xanthippou

Dinokrato

◉1

Cine Dexameni ●

Plateia
Dexameni

Glykonos

Spefsipo

24 🚇

21 🚇

Akadimias

Amerikis

Roma

Skoufa

Pindarou

Anagnostopoulou

Levendi

26 🔒

25

4

32 🔒

Numismatic
Museum

3 🔒 ✕14

Voukourestiou

Al Soutsou

Iraklitou

Milioni

18 🚇

Patriarhou Ioakein

KOLONA

5

27 🔒

31 🔒

Kriezotou

Zalokosta

Akadimias

30 🔒

Merlin

Kanari

Sekeri

Plateia
Kolonakiou

Depot Gallery
7 ◉

Kapsali

Neofytou Vamva

Irodotou

Neofytou Douka

◉2

Museum o
Cycladic A

23 🎭

Leof Vasilissis Sofias

11
✕ ◉

Benaki
Museum
of Greek
Culture

Koumbari

Mourouzi

Syntagma
Ⓜ

SYNTAGMA

National
Gardens

Leof Vasilissis Amalias

6

A

B

C

D

Kolonaki

Lykavittos Hill

E F G H

0 200 m
0 0.1 miles

Teleferik

Hoida

Doras D'Istria

Aristippou

Kleomenous

Dinokratous

Aheou

enokratous

Souidias

Haritos

Patriarhou Ioakeim

Alopekis

Karneadou

Ypsilandou

Karaoli-
Dimitriou

Aristotle's
Lyceum

Aristidimou

Iofliou

Xenokratous

Plateia
Dante

Kolonaki
Weekly Market

Athineon Efivon

Dimoharous

Dinokratous

Karahristou

Evzonon

Genadiou I

Iasiou

Ravine

Pateral

Marasli

Ploutarhou

Ypsilandou

Leof Vasilissis Sofias

Monis Petraki

Ventiri K

Ypsilandou

Evangelismos M

M Evangelismos

Plateia
Megalis tou
Genous Sholi

Leof Vas Konstantinou

War
Museum

Byzantine
& Christian
Museum

Rizari

🟡22

🟡15

10 🟡

🟡 9 8🟡

🔒29

🟡5

1🟡

4🟡

For reviews see	
🟡 Top Experiences	p100
🟡 Sights	p106
🟡 Eating	p108
🟡 Drinking	p110
⭐ Entertainment	p112
🔒 Shopping	p112

E F G H

1
2
3
4
5
6

Sights

Byzantine & Christian Museum

MUSEUM

1 ◉ MAP P104, E6

This outstanding museum does not look like much at first, but its exhibition halls lead one to the next in an expansive underground maze of glimmering gold and mosaics. The exhibits go chronologically, charting the gradual and fascinating shift from ancient traditions to Christian ones, and the flourishing of a distinctive Byzantine style. Of course there are icons, but also delicate frescoes (some salvaged from a church and installed on haunting floating panels) and more personal remnants of daily life. The villa grounds (free entry) are a series of formal gardens that include ancient ruins, such as a section of the 6th-century-BCE Peisistratos aqueduct. A pretty cafe overlooks the greenery. (☎213 213 9500; www.byzantinemuseum.gr; Leoforos Vasilissis Sofias 22, Kolonaki; adult/child €8/free; ☺noon-8pm Mon, from 8am Tue-Sun Apr-Oct, reduced hours Nov-Mar; ⓜEvangelismos)

Museum of Cycladic Art

MUSEUM

2 ◉ MAP P104, D5

The 1st floor of this exceptional private museum is dedicated to the iconic minimalist marble Cycladic figurines, dating from 3000 BCE to 2000 BCE. They inspired many 20th-century artists, such as Picasso and Modigliani, with their simplicity and purity of form. Most are surprisingly small, considering their outsize influence, though one is almost human size. The rest of the museum features Greek and Cypriot art dating from 2000 BCE to the 4th century CE. (☎210 722 8321; www.cycladic.gr; Neofytou Douka 4, cnr Leoforos Vasilissis Sofias, Kolonaki; adult/child €7/free, Mon half-price, special exhibits €10; ☺10am-5pm Mon, Wed, Fri & Sat, to 8pm Thu, 11am-5pm Sun; ⓜEvangelismos)

Numismatic Museum

MUSEUM

3 ◉ MAP P104, A4

The collection of coins here, dating from ancient times through to the Middle Ages, is excellent, but of more general interest is the dazzling 1881 mansion in which it's housed. Built by architect Ernst Ziller, it was the home of Heinrich Schliemann, the archaeologist who excavated Troy, and, fittingly, its mosaic floors and painted walls and ceilings are covered in classical motifs. The adjoining gardens have an excellent cafe. (☎210 363 2057; www.nummus.gr; Panepistimiou 12; adult/student €6/3; ☺8.30am-3.30pm Tue-Sun; ⓜPanepistimio, Syntagma)

War Museum

MUSEUM

4 ◉ MAP P104, F5

This relic of the junta years is an architectural statement of the times, bleak and grey. But its displays of weapons, maps, armour and models from the Mycenaean civilisation to the present day make an interesting break from the classics. Plus it's convenient if you're already at the nearby Byzantine Museum. (📞210 725 2975; www.warmuseum.gr; Rizari 2, cnr Leoforos Vasilissis Sofias, Kolonaki; adult/child €4/2; ⏰9am-7pm Apr-Oct, to 5pm Nov-Mar; Ⓜ️Evangelismos)

Aristotle's Lyceum   RUINS

5 ◎ MAP P104, E6

Excavated only in 2011, this site is not much to look at – only building outlines are visible – but it is hallowed ground. Aristotle founded his school here, outside the city walls, in 335 BCE. He taught rhetoric and philosophy, and the place became known as a Peripatetic

School, because teacher and pupils would walk as they talked. In the same way, you can make a circuit around the ruins. (Lykeion, Aristotle's School; http://odysseus. culture.gr; cnr Rigillis & Leoforos Vasilissis Sofias, Kolonaki; adult/child €4/free; ⏰8am-8pm Mon-Fri; Ⓜ️Evangelismos)

CAN   GALLERY

6 ◎ MAP P104, C3

The brainchild of Christina Androulidaki, this entry on the Kolonaki gallery scene has a stable of emerging contemporary Greek artists. In August it's open by appointment only. (📞210 339 0833; www.can-gallery.com; Anagnostopoulou 42, Kolonaki; ⏰11am-3pm & 5-8pm Tue-Fri, 11am-4pm Sat; Ⓜ️Syntagma)

Kolonaki Sights

Byzantine & Christian Museum

Byzantine Greece

The Byzantine Empire, which blended Hellenistic culture with Christianity, was established in CE 330, when the Roman emperor Constantine I, a Christian convert, declared the city of Byzantium the empire's new capital – and changed its name to his own: Constantinople. As Rome went into terminal decline, this eastern capital, the centre of a Christian state, grew in wealth and strength.

As for Greece, it became officially Christian a bit later, in 394, and the worship of Greek and Roman gods was banned. Athens managed to remain an important cultural centre until 529, when the teaching of 'pagan' classical philosophy was finally forbidden, in favour of Christian theology.

The Byzantine Empire faced continued pressure from the Persians and Arabs, but held the core of its territory for many centuries. Athens, though, was no longer a centre, but an edge, and it faced attacks from the west. Between 1200 and 1450, the city was occupied by a succession of opportunistic Franks, Catalans, Florentines and Venetians. The empire finally fell in 1453, when the Turks captured Constantinople – and changed its name again, to İstanbul. Dusty and neglected, Athens didn't regain any kind of status until 1834, when it was declared the capital of the new Greek state.

Depot Gallery
GALLERY

7 ◉ MAP P104, D5

This below-street-level space focuses on artists inspired by the urban environment (it sponsors the Athens Street Art Festival). Greek artists (including George Raptis, Vasilis Geros and Faye Tsakalides) and international names are on show; exhibitions change every two months or so. (☏210 364 8174; www.depotgallery.gr; Neofytou Vamva 5, Kolonaki; admission free; ⊗noon-9pm; ⓂEvangelismos)

Eating

Oikeio
MEDITERRANEAN €

8 ✕ MAP P104, E4

With excellent home-style cooking, this modern taverna lives up to its name (meaning 'homey'). It's decorated like a cosy bistro, and tables on the footpath allow people-watching without the usual Kolonaki bill. Pastas, salads and international fare are tasty, but try the daily mayirefta (ready-cooked meals), such as the excellent stuffed zucchini. Book ahead on weekends. (☏210 725 9216; Ploutarhou 15, Kolonaki; mains €8-12;

⊙12.30pm-midnight Mon-Thu, to 1am Fri & Sat, to 6pm Sun; **M** Evangelismos)

Kostarelos CHEESE €

9 ⊗ MAP P104, E4

Fun fact: Greeks eat the most dairy in Europe, an average of 30kg per person per year. And when you visit Kostarelos, you might see why. The long-established family dairy business is now an elegant little deli and sandwich shop that caters to cheese lovers in all ways, whether it's *saganaki* (fried cheese), fondue or creative sandwiches. (⏿ 210 725 9000; www.kostarelos.gr; Patriarhou Ioakeim 30, Kolonaki; sandwiches €5-7; ⊙8am-10pm Mon-Sat; **M** Evangelismos)

Kalamaki Kolonaki GREEK €

10 ⊗ MAP P104, E4

Order by the *kalamaki* (skewer; €1.70), add some salad and pittas, and you have great quick bites at this standout souvlaki joint. It's small, but there's pavement seating for the requisite people-watching. And, because it's Kolonaki, it's just a little more chic than average. (⏿ 210 721 8800; Ploutarhou 32, Kolonaki; mains €7; ⊙1pm-midnight; **M** Evangelismos)

Benaki Museum Cafe GREEK €€

11 ⊗ MAP P104, C5

Traditional Greek food gets dressed up to match the museum setting, with an open dining room and terrace with a view of the National Gardens and the Acropolis.

It feels a bit clubby, with older locals meeting for lunch, and it's open as late as the museum is, so you can have dinner or even just a late drink here. (Koumbari 1, Kolonaki; mains €12-16; ⊙9am-5pm Wed & Fri, to midnight Thu & Sat, to 4pm Sun; **M** Evangelismos)

Nice N' Easy CAFE €€

12 ⊗ MAP P104, B3

Dig into organic, fresh sandwiches, salads and brunch treats, such as huevos rancheros, beneath images of Louis Armstrong and Marilyn Monroe at this casual cafe. Lots of vegan and gluten-free options. (⏿ 210 361 7201; www.niceneasy.gr; Omirou 60, Kolonaki; mains €8-18; ⊙9am-1.30am; ⟋; **M** Panepistimio)

Papadakis SEAFOOD €€€

13 ⊗ MAP P104, C3

This understatedly chic restaurant, run by a well-known chef and cookbook author, specialises in traditional seafood, such as stewed octopus with honey and sweet wine, *salatouri* (fish salad) and sea salad (a type of green seaweed or sea asparagus). Service can be a bit snooty. (⏿ 210 360 8621; Fokylidou 15, Kolonaki; mains €18-38; ⊙1.30pm-midnight Mon-Sat, to 6pm Sun; **M** Syntagma)

Telemachos STEAK €€€

14 ⊗ MAP P104, A4

At this elegant, modern chophouse, gorgeous dry-aged Piedmontese beef is on display – but great only-in-Greece dishes such as spit-roasted lamb are on the menu, too. Grilling is done over charcoal, service is smooth, and classic Greek film music sets a retro tone. Don't be too daunted by the €75/kg steak; a set menu with lamb is just €24. (📞210 361 3300; www.telemachosathens.gr; Panepistimiou 10, Kolonaki; mains from €18; 🕙1pm-1am; Ⓜ Syntagma)

Capanna   ITALIAN €€

15 ✖ MAP P104, E4

Capanna hugs a corner, with tables wrapping around the footpath in summer. Cuisine is fresh Italian, from enormous pizzas to gnocchi with gorgonzola. Enjoy hearty eating with attentive service and a goblet of wine, although, this being Kolonaki, prices are a tad high. (📞210 724 1777; Ploutarhou 38, Kolonaki; mains €10-17; 🕙1pm-1am Tue-Sun; 🛜; Ⓜ Evangelismos)

Drinking

Jazz in Jazz   BAR

16 🅿 MAP P104, D3

A good cool-weather destination, this cosy bar glows with candles and vintage brass instruments, and stays warm with the sounds of New Orleans bebop and neighbours chatting over a glass of wine or whisky. (📞210 725 8362; Dinokratous 3, Kolonaki; 🕙8pm-3am; Ⓜ Syntagma, Evangelismos)

Dark Side of Chocolate   CAFE

17 🅿 MAP P104, A3

This tiny cafe in Kolonaki has made a name for itself for its

Bars on Tsakalof in Kolonaki

hot chocolate and handmade truffles, displayed like gems in a glass case. It's a tiny, cosy place for some restorative caffeine (as there's coffee, too) and a sweet to nibble. (210 339 2348; Solonos 49, Kolonaki; 8am-11pm Mon-Fri, from 10am Sat; M Panepistimio)

Da Capo   CAFE

18 MAP P104, C4

Da Capo anchors the cafes on Kolonaki's main square and is always mobbed. Unlike just about every other cafe in Greece, you have to order your coffee inside at the counter. (210 360 2497; Tsakalof 1, Kolonaki; 8am-7pm; M Syntagma)

Passepartout   BAR

19 MAP P104, B3

This all-day cafe-bar is archetypal slick Kolonaki: modern decor, comfy seating and a see-and-be-seen attitude. Outside tables fit the brunch set and by nightfall host a well-dressed crowd that spills on to the footpath. (210 364 5546; www.passepartoutcafe.gr; Skoufa 47, Kolonaki; 10am-2am; M Panepistimio)

Café Boheme   CAFE

20 MAP P104, A3

A jazzy, brasserie-like spot with a regular clientele of slightly older locals. By day it's quiet; later there might be a DJ and some singing

and dancing. It also has a great wine selection and good, fresh Greek food (mains €7 to €15). Not recommended if you're sensitive to cigarette smoke, though. (210 360 8018; www.cafeboheme.gr; Omirou 36, Kolonaki; 9.30am-3am, closed summer; M Panepistimiou)

Tsai   TEAHOUSE

21 MAP P104, B4

Get a Zen vibe as you sip tea at Japanese-minimalist blonde-wood tables. On a lively day a bit of Dixieland jazz may be tinkling in the background, and you might be moved to sit in one of the two playful swing seats. Light meals (€6 to €9) include soup and grilled chicken. (210 338 8941; www.tea.gr; Alexandrou Soutsou 19, Kolonaki; 6am-9pm Mon-Sat, daily winter; M Syntagma)

Prime
Plateia

Plateia Dexameni has basically everything you need: a great little cafe, a view of an ancient ruin (part of the cistern from Hadrian's aqueduct, dramatically lit at night) and the classic open-air **Cine Dexameni** (Map p104, D3; 210 362 3942; www.cinedexameni.gr; Plateia Dexameni, Kolonaki; adult/child €8/5, two-for-one Tue; M Evangelismos), which has deck chairs and tables to rest your beer on.

Entertainment

Cine Athinaia
CINEMA

22 ⭐ MAP P104, F3

This summer-only open-air cinema in Kolonaki is set at the end of a short pedestrian street of pleasant bars. (📞210 721 5717; www.cineathinaia.gr; Haritos 50, Kolonaki; adult/child €8/6, 2-for-1 Tue; Ⓜ Evangelismos)

Theocharakis Foundation for the Fine Arts & Music
ARTS CENTRE

23 ⭐ MAP P104, B5

This arts centre has a theatre that hosts classical music performances and other events, plus three levels of gallery space (€6; special exhibits change once or twice a year), an art shop and a pleasant cafe. (📞210 361 1206; www.thf.gr; Leoforos Vasilissis Sofias 9, Kolonaki; adult/child €6/free; ⏲10am-6pm Mon-Wed & Fri-Sun, to 8pm Thu Sep-Jul; 🛜; Ⓜ Syntagma)

Shopping

Lemisios
SHOES

24 🅰 MAP P104, B3

An Athens classic, open since 1912, with classic designs – T-straps, ballet flats, elegant Oxfords – all custom-fit just for you. Bespoke designs are also possible. Considering the level of craft, this place is surprisingly affordable. (📞210 361 1161; Lykavittou 6, Kolonaki; ⏲9am-

3pm Mon, Wed & Sat, to 8.30pm Tue, Thu & Fri; Ⓜ Syntagma, Panepistimio)

Katerina Ioannidis
JEWELLERY

25 🅰 MAP P104, C4

From a family of goldsmiths, Ioannidis merges Greek and other global folkloric elements into jewellery that is light, bohemian, sometimes even a little funny: a pendant of, say, a gold-plated sheep's head set on a fuzzy black pompom, or a bean-shaped charm. (📞6932375717; www.katerinaioannidis.com; Anagnosto-poulou 15, Kolonaki; ⏲10am-4pm Mon, Wed & Sat, to 9pm Tue, Thu & Fri; Ⓜ Syntagma)

Elena Votsi
JEWELLERY

26 🅰 MAP P104, D4

Votsi is renowned for her big and bold designs using exquisite semi-precious stones. So sculptural is her work that she was selected to design the 2004 Olympic Games medals, and she has branched out into handwoven bags and Greek-themed home items. In summer the Athens shop closes and she relocates to Hydra. (📞210 360 0936; www.elenavotsi.com; Xanthou 7, Kolonaki; ⏲10am-8pm Tue-Sat Oct-Mar; Ⓜ Evangelismos)

Mastiha Shop
FOOD

27 🅰 MAP P104, A5

Mastic, the medicinal resin from rare trees found only on the island of Chios, is the key ingredient in everything in this store, from natural skin products to a liqueur that's divine when served chilled. There's also an airport branch. (📞 210 363 2750; www.mastihashop.com; Panepistimiou 6, Syntagma; ⏰ 9am-8pm Mon & Wed, to 9pm Tue, Thu & Fri, to 5pm Sat; Ⓜ Syntagma)

Parthenis   FASHION & ACCESSORIES

28 🔒 MAP P104, C3

A father-daughter team designs these high-quality, supersleek clothes in natural fibres. No frills, just sharp lines. For both men and women. (📞 210 363 3158; www.orsalia-parthenis.gr; Dimokritou 20, cnr Tsakalof, Kolonaki; ⏰ 10am-3pm Mon & Wed, to 8.30pm Tue, Thu & Fri, to 4pm Sat; Ⓜ Syntagma)

Fanourakis   JEWELLERY

29 🔒 MAP P104, E4

One of the most creative and exciting Greek jewellers, Fanourakis designs delicate, quirky pieces: gold folded like pencil shavings, unicycle charms, pavé diamond rings like jagged rocks. The distinctive forms are sheer art. (📞 210 721 1762; www.fanourakis.gr; Patriarhou Ioakeim 23, Kolonaki; ⏰ 10am-5pm Mon, Wed & Sat, to 9pm Tue, Thu & Fri; Ⓜ Syntagma)

Vassilis Zoulias   FASHION & ACCESSORIES

30 🔒 MAP P104, B5

Greece's answer to Manolo Blahnik, Zoulias specialises in elegant, feminine shoes that are timeless in their style. His couture line continues this theme, with colourful dresses inspired by the '50s and '60s. (📞 210 338 9924; www.vassiliszoulias.com; Akadimias 4, Kolonaki; ⏰ 10am-5pm Mon, Wed & Sat, to 9pm Tue, Thu & Fri; Ⓜ Syntagma)

Zoumboulakis Gallery   ART

31 🔒 MAP P104, A5

An excellent selection of limited-edition prints and posters by leading Greek artists, including Yannis Tsarouchis, Dimitris Mytaras and Alekos Fassianos. The curators also have a contemporary space on the *plateia* in Kolonaki. (📞 210 363 4454; www.zoumboulakis.gr; Kriezotou 6, Syntagma; ⏰ 10am-3pm Mon & Wed, to 8pm Tue, Thu & Fri, 11am-4pm Sat; Ⓜ Syntagma)

Kombologadiko   FASHION

32 🔒 MAP P104, A4

If you're in the market for a very special set of that old-school Greek accessory, *komboloï* (worry beads), check this oh-so-elegant showroom. It stocks ready-made designs, some from semiprecious stones and amber, and can string custom sets from its collection of beads. (📞 212 700 0500; Amerikis 9, Kolonaki; ⏰ 10am-4pm Mon, Wed & Sat, to 9pm Tue, Thu & Sat; Ⓜ Syntagma)

Explore ⊗

Mets & Pangrati

East of the Acropolis, the Zappeio Gardens and the ruins of the Temple of Olympian Zeus lead to the elegant Panathenaic Stadium. On the hill above the stadium are the diverse, unpretentious districts of Mets and Pangrati, with some lovely neoclassical and prewar houses and low-key-cool places to eat.

The Temple of Olympian Zeus (p116) covers a large area, but you only need about half an hour or 45 minutes to stroll around. Likewise the Panathenaic Stadium (p120), where what you see is pretty much what you get. Still, if you've ever been competitive, it's a thrill to be on the track. Afterward, head uphill to relax on Plateia Varnava, then wander over to Athens' First Cemetery (p121), where Greek luminaries are buried in elaborate tombs. Pangrati has two destination restaurants, Spondi (pictured; p122) and Mavro Provato (p122). The former is on the dressy side, so tricky to combine with earlier sightseeing. Make a separate trip (taxis are cheap, remember), and possibly combine it with a show at Half Note Jazz Club (p124) or a film at Aegli Cinema (p125).

Getting There & Around

Ⓜ Akropoli (red line) or Syntagma (blue and red lines) for the Temple of Olympian Zeus. Akropoli is closest to Mets.

🚃 Trolleybus 2, 4 or 11; these stop near the stadium and continue uphill to Plateia Plastira.

🚋 Consider Mets an excuse to ride the tram one stop. Get off at Zappeio.

Neighbourhood Map on p118

Temple of Olympian Zeus (p103)

Top Experience

Marvel at the Temple of Olympian Zeus

You can't miss this marvel, smack in the centre of Athens. In terms of ground area it is the largest temple in Greece. It was probably also one of the most drawn-out projects in history, begun in the 6th century BCE and finished in CE 131.

◉ MAP P118, A3

Olympieio

http://odysseus.culture.gr

Leoforos Vasilissis Olgas

adult/student/child €6/3/free

🕒 8am-3pm Oct-Apr, to 8pm May-Sep

Ⓜ Akropoli, Syntagma

Temple

Seven centuries after Peisistratos started, Hadrian finished the temple by placing a giant gold-and-ivory statue of Zeus inside. Then he matched it with an equally large one of himself. Maybe his immodesty jinxed it: the very next century, the temple was destroyed when the Herulians (a Germanic tribe from near the Black Sea) sacked the city.

Columns

The temple was built with 104 Corinthian columns, each with a base diameter of 1.7m and standing 17m high. Only 15 remain, the rest having been repurposed over the centuries, so you'll have to squint to imagine the whole scope of the temple. The one fallen column was blown down in a gale in 1852.

Original Temple

Hadrian's temple is built on the site of a smaller one (590–560 BCE), also dedicated to the cult of Olympian Zeus. Look closely: its foundations can still be seen.

Hadrian's Arch

Just outside the temple fence, at the corner of Leoforos Vasilissis Amalias, sits this lofty monument, erected as thanks to Roman emperor Hadrian, probably just after the temple was consecrated. The inscriptions laud the new Roman era: the northwest frieze reads, 'This is Athens, the Ancient city of Theseus', while the southeast frieze states, 'This is the city of Hadrian, and not of Theseus'.

Sanctuary of Pan

Outside the temple fence to the south explorers can find a slip of the Ilissos River (elsewhere covered by pavement) and, nearby, a rock-cut sanctuary to the god Pan, another Roman-era worship site. Look for it near a church at the corner of Ardittou and Athanasiou Diakou.

★ Top Tips

o Admission to the site is included in the €30 Acropolis combo ticket.

o There is no shade: wear a hat and sunscreen and bring water.

o You can see most of the temple (and Hadrian's Arch) from outside the fence if you're rushed. Or peer down on it all from the rooftop bar at the **Athens Gate** (210 923 8302; www.athensgate.gr; Leoforos Syngrou Andrea 10, Makrygianni; M Akropoli) hotel.

✕ Take a Break

For a shady rest and a light snack, head to the Zappeio Gardens' Aegli Cafe (p124). Or walk up to Mets for a laid-back coffee at the Odeon Cafe (p124) and a spinach pie from the excellent bakery across the street.

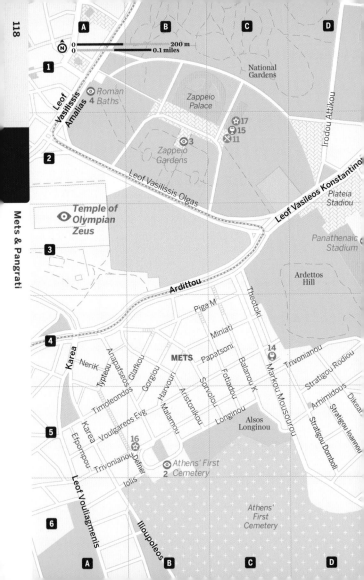

Mets & Pangrati

N
0   200 m
0   0.1 miles

A B C D

1

National
Gardens

Leof Vasilissis Amalias

Roman
4 Baths

Zappeio
Palace

Zappeio
Gardens

3

17
15
11

2

Leof Vasilissis Olgas

Leof Vasileos Konstantinou

Plateia
Stadiou

Temple of
Olympian
Zeus

3

Panathenaic
Stadium

Ardettos
Hill

Ardittou

Piga M

Theotoki

4

Karea

NeriK

Anapafseos

Glafkou

Gorgiou

Harvouri

Miniati

Papatsoni

Fotiadou

Balanou k

Aristonikou

Sorvolou

Markou Mousourou

Trivonianou

Stratigou Rodiou

Stratigou Ioannou

Arhimidous

Dikear

14

METS

Typteou

Timoleondos

Voulgareos Evg

Malamou

Longinou

Alsos
Longinou

Stratigou Domboli

5

Karea

Efpompou

Trivonianou

Defner

16

Iolis

Athens' First
2 Cemetery

6

Leof Voullagmenis

Ilioupoleos

Athens'
First
Cemetery

A B C D

E · F · G · H

🦷 13

For reviews see	
⦿ Top Experiences	p116
⊙ Sights	p120
✕ Eating	p122
🍷 Drinking	p124
★ Entertainment	p124
🛍 Shopping	p125

Leof Vasileos Konstantinou

Isiodou · Fokianou

6
✕

Telesilis
Polemonos

Ag. Spyridonos · Arktinou · Ironda
Patsaniou
Arrianou
Eilanikou

Efforionos · Ivikou

Fedrou

Basil & Elise Goulandris Foundation
⊙ **5**

Agras · Versi · Ktisiviou · Diotandou · Ironos

Theofrastou

Aristoxenou

Eratosthenous

Spyrou Merkouri

Tsiklitira

Ippodamou · Athanasias · Nikosthenous

Alsos Pangratiou

Douridos · Pratinou

Agras

Plateia Plastira

Eftyhidou

12 🍷

Arhimidou
10 ✕

Aratou

Lysippou

Pastelous

Effranoros

PANGRATI

Arhyta
9 ✕

eitomachou · Ferekydou · Embedokleous

Proklou · Pyrgotelous · Krisila · Tydeos

Vryaxidos

Frynis · Ymittou · Pyrrou

18 🛍

7 ✕ Plateia Varnava

Parmenidou

Melissou

Neoptolemou

Plateia Profitiou Ilia

Proeresiou · Stilponos

8 ✕

Korivou

Anarhidos

Anakreondos

Alketou

Stilponos · Epimitheos · Pyrronos

Edesiou · Ekalis

Embedokleous

Damareos · Argyvou

Dikearhou

Ymittou

Evmenous

Lysimahou

Neoptolemou

Filolaou

E · F · G · H

Sights

Panathenaic Stadium

HISTORIC SITE

1  MAP P118, D3

As an actual site to visit, this ancient-turned-modern stadium (pictured below) – built in the 4th century BCE, and restored for the first modern Olympic games in 1896 – will be most interesting to sports fans who can imagine the roar of the millennia-old crowds. A ticket gets you an audio tour, admission to a tiny exhibit on the modern Olympics and the opportunity to take your photo on a winners' pedestal. The stadium was first used as a venue for the Panathenaic athletic contests, and it's said that at Hadrian's inauguration

in CE 120, a thousand wild animals were sacrificed in the arena. Later, the seats were rebuilt in Pentelic marble by Herodes Atticus.

In 1895, after centuries of disuse, the stadium was restored by wealthy Greek benefactor Georgios Averof, as a faithful replica of the original. It seats 70,000 spectators around the running track and field – which is not, unfortunately, modern Olympic-size, so the stadium could be used only for archery and the marathon finish in the 2004 games. Now it's occasionally used for concerts and public events. (Kallimarmaro; ☎210 752 2984; www.panathenaicstadium.gr; Leoforos Vasileos Konstantinou, Pangrati; adult/student/child €5/2.50/free; ☺8am-7pm Mar-Oct, to 5pm

Panathenaic Stadium

Nov-Feb; 🚋2, 4, 10, 11 to Stadio, Ⓜ️Akropoli, 🚃Zappeio)

Athens' First Cemetery

CEMETERY

2 ◎ MAP P118, B5

Under Ottoman rule, Greeks buried their dead at their local church. Only after independence in 1821 was this city cemetery established. It's a peaceful place to explore, with beautiful neoclassical sculptures, including *Sleeping Maiden* by Yannoulis Chalepas, the most admired Greek sculptor of the modern era. Famous people buried here include the Benaki family and the archaeologist Heinrich Schliemann (1822–90), whose mausoleum is decorated with scenes from the Trojan War. (Longinou, Mets; admission free; 🕙8am-5pm winter, 7am-8pm summer; Ⓜ️Sygrou-Fix)

Zappeio Gardens

GARDENS

3 ◎ MAP P118, B2

The southwestern third of the green space at the centre of Athens, adjacent to the National Gardens (p82), is a network of wide, tree-shaded walkways around the grand **Zappeio Palace**. The palace was built in the 1870s and hosts conferences and exhibitions. A pleasant cafe, restaurant and the open-air Aegli Cinema (p125) are alongside the palace.

The main entrances are on Leoforos Vasilissis Amalias and Leoforos Vasilissis Olgas. (admission free; Ⓜ️Syntagma)

Morning Jog

There's no excuse not to exercise on your vacation: you can run laps or stairs in Olympic style at the **Panathenaic Stadium** from 7.30am to 9am every morning. Sign a waiver (download from the website), and you're good to go.

Roman Baths

RUINS

4 ◎ MAP P118, A1

Excavation work to create a ventilation shaft for the metro uncovered the well-preserved ruins of a large Roman bath complex, built in the 3rd century CE where the Ilissos River once ran. A portion is exposed at the edge of the Zappeio Gardens, and you can peer down from above. (Leoforos Vasilissis Amalias; admission free; Ⓜ️Syntagma)

Basil & Elise Goulandris Foundation

MUSEUM

5 ◎ MAP P118, E2

Opened in October 2019, this new museum showcases the collection of modern and contemporary artworks belonging to shipping magnate Basil Goulandris and his wife Elise. Alongside pieces from the likes of top European artists including Cézanne, Van Gogh, Picasso and Giacometti are works from pioneering Greek painters such as Parthenis, Vasiliou, Hadjikyriakos-

Peisistratos the Dictator

The first seeds of Athenian democracy were sown when Solon became *arhon* (chief magistrate) in 594 BCE and improved the lot of the poor by forgiving debts and establishing a process of trial by jury.

This initial foray did not last, however. The reforms provoked unrest, and on the pretext of restoring stability, Peisistratos, head of the military, seized power in 560 BCE. He focused not on the people, but on Athenian might, building a formidable navy and extending the city's influence. He began work on the Temple of Olympian Zeus, built a massive aqueduct and inaugurated the Festival of the Great Dionysia, the precursor to Attic drama.

In 528 BCE, Peisistratos was succeeded by his son, Hippias, no less an oppressor. With the help of Sparta in 510 BCE, Athens rid itself of him, and entered into its golden age of philosophy, arts and, again, democracy.

Ghikas, Tsarouchis and Moralis. (📞210 725 2895; www.goulandris.gr; Eratosthenous 13, Pangrati; Ⓜ Akropoli)

Eating

Mavro Provato
MEZEDHES €

6 ✖ MAP P118, G1

Book ahead for this wildly popular modern *mezedhopoleio* (mezedhes restaurant) in Pangrati, where tables line the footpath and delicious small (well, small for Greece) plates are paired with regional Greek wines. (Black Sheep; 📞210 722 3466; www.tomauroprovato.gr; Arrianou 31, Pangrati; dishes €5-12; ⏱noon-midnight Mon-Sat; Ⓜ Evangelismos)

Kallimarmaro
BAKERY €

7 ✖ MAP P118, F5

Exceptionally good *spanakopita* (spinach pie) and other pies at this neighbourhood bakery – it's the breakfast go-to for many locals. Fills all your cream-puff needs too. (📞210 701 9062; Plateia Varnava 22, Pangrati; pita €2; ⏱8am-8pm Mon-Sat; 🚌209 to Plateia Varnava)

Spondi
MEDITERRANEAN €€€

8 ✖ MAP P118, F5

Athenians frequently vote two-Michelin-starred Spondi the city's best restaurant, and its Mediterranean haute cuisine, with a strong French influence, is indeed excellent. Visitors to the city might want something a bit more distinctly Greek, however. Either way, it's a lovely dining experience, in a relaxed setting in a charming old house with a bougainvillea-draped garden. Book ahead. (📞210 756 4021; www.spondi.gr; Pyrronos 5, Pangrati; mains €47-60, set menus from €73; ⏱8pm-late; 🚌209 to Plateia Varnava, 🚋2, 4 or 11 to Plateia Plastira)

Colibri

PIZZA €

9 🦊 MAP P118, F4

One of several fine cafes on this quiet, tree-lined street, but locals go here for the alleged best pizza in Athens, served to a low-key reggae soundtrack. The pies range from classic Italian to creative vegetarian (seriously, the yoghurt works). Burgers and salads are also excellent. (📞210 701 1011; Embedokleous 9-13, Pangrati; small pizzas €6-12, mains €5-9; ⏰1pm-12.30am; 🚌2, 4, 11 to Plateia Plastira)

Vyrinis

TAVERNA €

10 🦊 MAP P118, F4

Just behind the old Panathenaic stadium, this popular neighbourhood spot has been modernised a bit, but maintains its essential taverna-ness, with home-style Greek food and reliable house wine at reasonable prices. On warm nights, all activity moves to the lovely courtyard garden, just up the side street. (📞210 701 2153; Arhimidous 11, Pangrati; mains €6-8; ⏰7-11pm Mon-Wed, 1-11pm Thu-Sun; 🚌2, 4, 11 to Plateia Plastira)

Aegli Restaurant

MEZEDHES €

11 🦊 MAP P118, C2

Smack in the heart of the green Zappeio Gardens (p121) and next to the palace, this place doesn't do the most inspired food, but it's convenient if you're going to the adjacent outdoor cinema. It's popular for traditional mezedhes and mains, which range from dolmades to marinated anchovies or mushroom risotto. In summer aim

Athens' First Cemetery (p121)

for the alfresco tables. (📞210 336 9364; www.aeglizappiou.gr; Zappeio Gardens; mezedhes €5-9; ⏰1pm-1am; Ⓜ️Syntagma, Akropoli)

Drinking

Chelsea Hotel BAR

12 🚇 MAP P118, F3

When people talk about the cool but mellow scene in Pangrati, they're probably thinking of this busy cafe-bar on Plateia Plastira. By day it's coffee, books and the occasional laptop. When the sun sets every seat, inside and out, is filled with young Athenians aspiring to be as artistic and bohemian as residents of the bar's NYC namesake. (📞210 756 3374; Arhimidous 1, cnr Proklou, Pangrati; ⏰8am-late; 🛜; 🚌2, 4, 11 to Plateia Plastira)

Epireia CAFE

13 🚇 MAP P118, F1

One of several nice cafes on a pretty green square, this airy, colourful place has the typical unpretentious Pangrati vibe, plus solid food (pizza, burgers) and craft beers. It's a bit of a walk from public transport, but it makes a nice endpoint if you've been wandering the neighbourhood. (📞210 725 4594; Ktisiou 2, Pangrati; ⏰11am-1am Mon-Thu, to 3am Fri, 10.30am-3am Sat, to 1am Sun; 🚌2, 4, 11 to Stadio, Ⓜ️Evangelismos)

Odeon Cafe CAFE

14 🚇 MAP P118, C4

This corner cafe-bar is a delightful slice of local Athens life: friends chat quietly beneath an ivy bower over the footpath. Extra-friendly staff, plus snacks and drinks, and occasional live music at night. (📞210 922 3414; Markou Mousourou 19, Mets; ⏰8.30am-2am Sun-Thu, to 3am Fri & Sat; Ⓜ️Akropoli)

Aegli Cafe BAR

15 🚇 MAP P118, C2

A stylish and cool (literally) cafe-bar-restaurant set among the trees in the middle of the Zappeio Gardens (p121), with comfy loungers and ever-changing decor. It's a low-key cafe by day, while at night it boasts mainstream music and a slick crowd. Note that the food is not the draw. (📞210 336 9340; Zappeio Gardens; ⏰9am-midnight; Ⓜ️Syntagma)

Entertainment

Half Note Jazz Club JAZZ

16 ⭐ MAP P118, B5

Athens' most serious jazz venue is a stylish place that hosts Greek and international musicians. Check the schedule ahead of your trip, as it's not open every night and closes entirely in summer. (📞210 921 3310; www.halfnote.gr; Trivonianou 17, Mets; Ⓜ️Akropoli)

Olympic History

The Olympic tradition emerged at the site of Olympia in the Peloponnese around the 11th century BCE as a paean to Zeus. Initially, it was footraces only, run by priests, priestesses and other notables. By the 8th century BCE, the festival had morphed into a major, male-only event that convened for five days every four years; the schedule alternated years with other regional competitions around Greece, a cycle referred to as the Panhellenic Games. This way, athletes could compete frequently. During the competition, city-states were bound by a sacred truce to stop any fighting underway.

Crowds of spectators lined the tracks, where competitors vied for victory in athletics, chariot races, wrestling and boxing. Unlike at Athens' Panathenaic contests, where winners received cash and valuable olive oil, the first prize at the Olympic games was purely symbolic: a simple crown of olive leaves. (Laurel wreaths, now considered a symbol of victory, were awarded at the Pythian Games, one of the other regional competitions.) Ultimately, it was the esteem of the people that most mattered, for Greek Olympians were venerated. The ancient games ceased in CE 393, when Emperor Theodosius I banned all pagan worship, and were revived in modern form in 1896.

Aegli Cinema
CINEMA

17 ⭐ MAP P118, C2

The historic open-air cinema showed its first film in 1903. Set in the verdant Zappeio Gardens (p121), it's a little quieter than others. (📞210 336 9369; www.aegli zappiou.gr; Zappeio Gardens; adult/child €8.50/6.50; ⊘screenings at 9pm & 11pm May-Oct; MSyntagma)

Shopping

Bakaliko
FOOD & DRINKS

18 🅰 MAP P118, F4

A one-stop shop for fine Greek food products, this store is decked with awards for its dedication and stock of traditional oil, wine, cheese, nuts, yoghurt and honey. Herbs hang in bunches, lentils fill sacks, beans are dazzling in their freshness and variety. (📞210 756 0055; Proklou 31, Pangrati; ⊘9am-3pm Mon, Tue & Sat, to 6pm Wed, Thu & Fri; 🚌2, 4, 11 to Plateia Plastira)

Explore ⬡

Omonia & Exarhia

Omonia is Athens' practical centre, a transport hub and the location of key administrative offices. It's not a destination, but you'll inevitably pass through – perhaps on your way to neighbouring Exarhia and the National Archaeological Museum. Exarhia is most famous for its squat scene and its vocal anarchists, but it's an interesting mix of students (it's near the universities), artists, immigrants, families and old lefties, against a backdrop of graffiti and occasional riot police.

The National Archaeological Museum (p128) can easily fill a half-day; if you still have a little energy, duck into the Epigraphical Museum (p137) around the corner. Afterward, lunch in Exarhia at student-casual Kimatothrafstis (p139), or head to Plateia Omonias for a coffee break at the grand cafe Veneti (p141).

To dig deeper in Exarhia, stroll side streets in search of murals, collectors' shops and new designers like Zacharias. When evening comes, the neighbourhood rewards bar-hopping and snacking, and the music scene is great and diverse, at places like Feidiou 2 Music Cafe (p143) and AN Club (p144).

Getting There & Around

Ⓜ Omonia (red and green lines) sits due west of Exarhia.

Ⓜ Panepistimio (red line) for southern Exarhia.

🚌 Trolleybus 2, 4, 5, 9 or 11 from anywhere on Panepistimiou to Polytechnio stop, in front of the archaeological museum.

Neighbourhood Map on p136

National Theatre (p143) TONY_TRAVELER85/SHUTTERSTOCK ©

Top Experience 📷
Admire Antiquities at the National Archaeological Museum

The National Archaeological Museum houses the world's finest collection of Greek antiquities. The enormous 19th-century neoclassical building holds room upon room, filled with more than 10,000 examples of sculpture, pottery, jewellery, frescoes and more. You simply can't appreciate it all in one go – but whatever you do lay eyes on will be a treat.

◎ MAP P136, D1

www.namuseum.gr

Patision 44, Exarhia

adult/child €10/free

⊙ 1-8pm Mon, 8am-8pm Tue-Sun, reduced hours in winter

🚌 2, 3, 4, 5 or 11 to Poly-technio, Ⓜ Viktoria

Mycenaean Antiquities

GALLERY 4

Directly ahead as you enter the museum is the prehistoric collection, showcasing some of the most important pieces of Mycenaean, neolithic and Cycladic art, many in solid gold. The fabulous collection of Mycenaean antiquities is the museum's tour de force.

Mask of Agamemnon

This great death mask of beaten gold is commonly known as the Mask of Agamemnon, the king who, according to legend, attacked Troy in the 12th century BCE – but this is hardly certain. Heinrich Schliemann, the archaeologist who set to prove that Homer's epics were true tales, and not just myth, unearthed the mask at Mycenae in 1876. But now some archaeologists have found the surrounding grave items date from centuries earlier. And one researcher even asserts that Schliemann, a master of self-promotion, forged it completely.

Vaphio Cups

The exquisite Vaphio gold cups, with scenes of men taming wild bulls, are regarded as among the finest surviving examples of Mycenaean art. They were found in a *tholos* (Mycenaean tomb shaped like a beehive) at Vaphio, near Sparta.

Cycladic Collection

GALLERY 6

This room contains some of the superbly minimalist marble figurines of the 3rd and 2nd millennia BCE that inspired artists such as Picasso. One splendid example measures 1.52m and dates from 2600 to 2300 BCE.

Sounion Kouros

GALLERY 8

The galleries to the left of the entrance house the oldest and most significant pieces of the sculpture collection. Galleries 7 to 13 exhibit

★ Top Tips

○ A joint museum ticket is available for €15 (€8 for students), valid for three days here and at the neighbouring Epigraphical Museum, plus the Byzantine & Christian Museum and the Numismatic Museum.

○ Arrive early in the day to beat the rush. If you come after tour groups are moving through, head upstairs first.

○ Allow a few hours, and maybe more if you have a special interest.

○ Exhibits are displayed largely thematically. For more information get an audioguide.

✗ Take a Break

The **museum cafe** in the basement extends into an open-air internal courtyard.

For a meal, head into Exarhia, to a place like Yiantes (p139) for fresh modern Greek food with a glass of wine.

fine examples of Archaic *kouroi* (male statues) from the 7th century BCE to 480 BCE. The most interesting is the colossal 600 BCE Sounion Kouros, which stood before the Temple of Poseidon at Sounio. Its style marks a transition point in art history, starting with the rigid lines of older Egyptian carving but also showing some of the life-like qualities – including the so-called 'Archaic smile' – that the Greeks would perfect in later centuries.

Artemision Bronze

GALLERY 15

This room is dominated by the incredibly precise, just-larger-than-life bronze statue of Zeus or Poseidon (no one really knows which), excavated from the sea off Evia in 1928. The muscled figure, which dates from 460 BCE, has an iconic bearded face and holds his arms outstretched, his right hand raised to throw what was once a lightning bolt (if Zeus) or trident (if Poseidon).

Varvakeion Athena

GALLERY 20

Admire the details on this statue of Athena, made in CE 200: the helmet topped with a sphinx and griffins, a Gorgon shield and the hand holding a small figure of winged Nike (missing its head). Now imagine it all more than 10 times larger and covered in gold – that was the legendary, now-lost colossal figure of Athena (11.5m tall) that the master sculptor Pheidias erected in front of the Parthenon in the 5th century BCE. This daintier version is thought to be the best extant replica of that colossus.

Statue of Aphrodite, Eros and Pan

National Archaeological Museum

1st Floor

Cypriot Collection

Pottery Collection •

Pottery Collection •

Panathenaic Amphorae

Lift

Thira Gallery

Akrotiri Frescoes •

Egyptian Gallery

Stathatos Collection

Lift

Temporary Exhibitions

Jockey of Artemision •

Statue of Aphrodite •

Artemision Bronze •

Vaphio Gold Cups •

Lift

Varvakeion Athena •

Prehistoric Collection

Mycenaean Antiquities •

Mask of Agamemnon •

Cycladic Collection •

Sounion Kouros •

Ground Floor

Entrance

Lift

Cafe

Toilets

Museum Shop

Basement

Jockey of Artemision

Jockey of Artemision

GALLERY 21

This is another find from the ship-wreck off Evia excavated in 1928. This delicately rendered bronze horse and rider dates from the 2nd century BCE; only a few parts were found at first, and it was finally reassembled in 1972. Opposite the horse are several lesser-known but equally exquisite works, such as the statue of a demure nude **Aphrodite** struggling to hold her draped gown over herself.

Antikythera Shipwreck

GALLERY 28

Precious treasures discovered in 1900 by sponge divers off the island of Antikythera include the striking bronze **Antikythera Youth**, forged in the 4th century BCE. His hand once held some spherical object, now lost. More mysterious is the **Antikythera Mechanism**, an elaborate clockwork device, now in fragments, apparently for calculating astronomical positions as well as dates of eclipses and the Olympic games, among other events. Who made it, and when, is still unknown.

Egyptian Galleries

GALLERIES 40 AND 41

Two rooms present the best of the museum's significant Egyptian collection, the only one in Greece. Dating from 5000 BCE to the Roman conquest, artefacts include mummies, bronze figurines and beautifully evocative Roman-era painted portraits from caskets (so-called Fayum portraits).

Akrotiri Frescoes

GALLERY 48

Upstairs a room is devoted to the spectacular and incredibly old Minoan frescoes from a prehistoric settlement on Santorini (Thira). The frescoes were preserved when they were buried by a volcanic eruption in the late 16th century BCE. The frescoes include *Boxing Children* and *Spring,* depicting red lilies and a pair of swallows kissing in mid air. The Thira Gallery also has videos showing the 1926 eruption and the Akrotiri excavation.

Pottery Collection

GALLERY 55

The superb pottery collection traces the development of pottery from the Bronze Age through the Protogeometric and Geometric periods, to the famous **Attic black-figured pottery** (6th century BCE), and **red-figured pottery** (late 5th to early 4th centuries BCE). Other uniquely Athenian vessels are the **Attic White Lekythoi**, slender vases depicting scenes at tombs.

The Museum Building

o The museum took shape between 1866 and 1889, with a facade designed by Ernst Ziller, a prolific architect who helped shape Athens' late-19th-century neoclassical style. He also designed the National Theatre (p143) and the mansion that is now the Numismatic Museum (p106).

o The east wing expanded during the 20th century.

o All told, the museum has about 8000 sq metres of floor space.

Panathenaic Amphorae

GALLERY 56

This room displays some of the ceramic vases presented to the winners of the Panathenaic Games. Each one contained oil from the sacred olive trees of Athens; victors might have received up to 140 of them. The vases are painted with scenes from the relevant sport (wrestling, in this case) on one side and an armed Athena *promachos* (champion) on the other.

Walking Tour 🚶

Neighbourhood Life in Exarhia

On the one hand, Exarhia is known for its anti-capitalist politics and its squatted buildings; on the other, it has loads of thriving little shops, especially for collectors' items and books, and publishing houses. After dinner, the bar scene is distinctly casual and student-friendly, with plenty of live music waiting to be stumbled upon.

Walk Facts

Start Plateia Exarhion

Finish Emmanuel Benaki and Valtetsiou

Length 1.5km; one hour

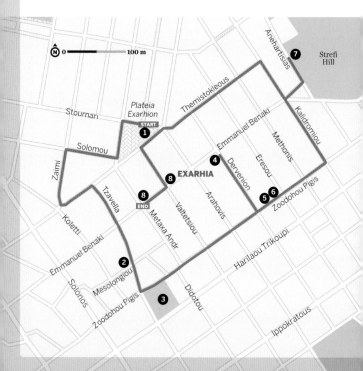

❶ Plateia Exarhion

This square (triangle, really) is the centre of neighbourhood life, and there is very often some political event taking place. Pick a spot for prime people-watching – any of the cafes on Themistokleous, or, at a slight remove but with a view downhill, **Ivi** (p141) on Stournari.

❷ Streets as Galleries

The walls, alleys and stairways of Exarhia are adorned with some of the world's most creative street art, often with a pointed underlying political message. At the corner of Mesolongiou and Tzavella is a **memorial for Alexis Grigoropoulos**, the teen whose 2008 death inspired riots across Greece.

❸ Reclaimed Square

In 2009 the inhabitants of Exarhia claimed most of a city block, formerly a parking lot, to use as a green space. Now **Navarino Park** (cnr Navarinou & Zoodohou Pigis; admission free; M Omonia) has a playground and fruit trees, and it's still all planted and maintained locally, and always developing.

❹ Old-World Taverna

Lunch at Exarhia institution **Barbagiannis** (p140). Choose from the variety of big trays of traditional dishes behind the counter, such as *pastitsio* (layers of baked macaroni and minced meat), washed down with house wine.

❺ Record Shopping

Exarhia's fun and super-niche shops include the chance to pick up, among other things, old-school vinyl. Serious music fans comb **Plan 59** (p144), for instance, for vintage Greek psychedelia.

❻ Buy Nothing

The secondhand shop **Skoros** (📞 6985868544; Eresou 33; ⏰ 6-8.30pm Mon-Fri, also 11.30am-2pm Mon & Wed, 12.30-5pm Sat; M Omonia) represents Exarhia's community spirit: there's no money involved. The policy is 'give what you can, take what you like.'

❼ Head for the Hill

Strefi Hill, up the (graffiti-bedecked) stairs on the northeast side of the neighbourhood, is where residents congregate around sundown. Have a beer at **Exostrefis** (p142).

❽ Go Cretan for Dinner

Neighbourhood denizens love **Rakoumel** (📞 210 380 0506; www.facebook.com/rakumel/; Emmanuel Benaki 71; dishes €5-9; ⏰ 1pm-2.30am Mon-Sat; 🛜; M Omonia) and **Oxo Nou** (📞 210 380 1778; www.facebook.com/oxonouathens; Emmanuel Benaki 63-65; mains €8-11; ⏰ 1pm-1.30am; 🛜; M Omonia) for their super Cretan food, featuring mountain herbs and slow-cooked meats. These lively restaurants are just a block apart, so you could sample small plates at both.

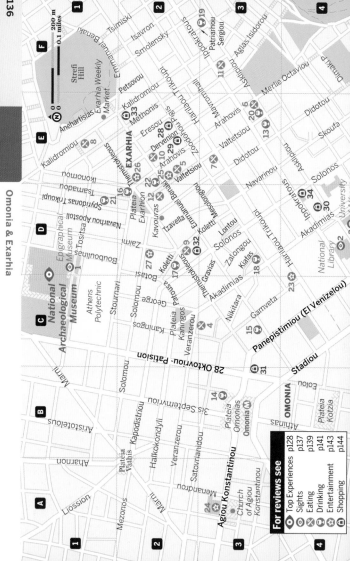

Omonia & Exarhia

F **E** **D** **C** **B** **A**

0 200 m
0.1 miles
N

Strefi Hill

Emmanuel Benaki

Tsimiski

Isavron

Smolensky

Patriarhou
Sergiou

⊗19

Hippokratous

Agias Isidorou

Dinaki P

Exarhia Weekly Market

Anehartisias

Kalidromiou

Petsovou

⊗11

Merlie Octaviou

Didotou

Kalidromiou

⊗8

Methonis

Eresou

Kalidromiou

Haritos Trikoupi

Zoodohou Pigis

EXARHIA
⊗33

⊗26

Derenion

Arahovis

Askliptou

Arahovis

⊗6
⊗20
⊗13

Mavromihali

Valtetsiou

Didotou

Skoufa

Ikonomou

Tsamadou

Spyridonos Trikoupi

⊗16
⊗21

⊗22

⊗25

⊗10

⊗29

Arahovis

⊗5

Valtetsiou

Navarinou

Askliptou

Solonos

Epigraphical Museum
⊗1

Navarhou Apostoli

Plateia
Exarhion
⊗12

Kavouras

Emmanuel Benaki

Tzavella

Mesolongiou

⊗7

⊗34

University

Bouboulinas

Tositsa

Zaimi

Koletti

Lontou

Solonos

Zalongou

Akadimias

National
Library
⊗2

National
Archaeological
Museum ⊗1

Epigraphical Museum

Themistokleous

Koletti

Gravias

Kiafas

⊗23

Athens Polytechnic

Botasi

Stournari

George

Perousa

⊗27

⊗9

⊗17

⊗32

Akadimias

⊗18

Solomou

Kaningos

Plateia
Kaningos

Nikitara

Gariveta

Panepistimiou (El Venizelou)

Marni

Aharnon

Aristotelous

Kapodistriou

Halkokondyli

Veranzerou

28 Oktovriou-Patision

⊗15

⊗31

Panepistimiou

Stadiou

Eolou

OMONIA

Liossion

Mezonos

Marni

Satovrianidou

Menandron

3is Septemvriou

Veranzerou

⊗14

Plateia
Vathis

Plateia
Omonias
Omonia Ⓜ

Agiou Konstantinou

Church
of Agiou
Konstantinou

⊗24

Plateia
Kotzia

Athinas

For reviews see	
◉ Top Experiences	p128
◉ Sights	p137
✖ Eating	p139
◉ Drinking	p141
◉ Entertainment	p143
◉ Shopping	p144

1 **2** **3** **4**

Sights

Epigraphical Museum   MUSEUM

1 ⊙ MAP P136, D1

On the south side of the National Archaeological Museum, this is an important collection of Greek inscriptions, but the main halls' tersely labelled shelves of stones are uninspiring to the casual visitor. Two newer sections, however, give some background on the Greek writing system and show off the most historically revealing pieces, such as a third-century copy (or perhaps forgery) of the decree ordering the evacuation of Athens before the 480 BCE Persian invasion. (☏ 210 821 7637; http://odysseus.culture.gr; Tositsa 1, Exarhia; €4; ⊙ 8am-3pm Tue-Sun; ☐ 2, 3, 4, 5, or 11 to Polytechneio, Ⓜ Viktoria)

National Library   HISTORIC BUILDING

2 ⊙ MAP P136, D4

One of a so-called neoclassical trilogy of buildings on Panepistimiou, the 1888 National Library is a dazzling construction by Danish architect Theophil Hansen, who also designed the Athens Academy, two buildings south. Unfortunately it's closed to the public, as the library's holdings – such as an original codex of the Gospel of Matthew and a vast collection of theatre archives – have been transferred to the Stavros Niarchos Foundation Cultural Center (p171). Still, the grand staircase makes a good photo op. (☏ 210 338 2541; www.nlg.gr; Panepistimiou 32, Panepistimio; admission free; ⊙ closed to the public; Ⓜ Panepistimio)

National Library

Exarhia's Political Legacy

Exarhia's anarchic reputation developed in the dark years of Greece's military junta. More recently, the neighbourhood – and the nation – was freshly galvanised by a brutal killing by police.

The Athens Polytechnic Uprising

On 21 April 1967 a group of army colonels staged a coup and installed one of their own, Georgios Papadopoulos, as prime minister. The regime declared martial law, banned political parties and trade unions, imposed censorship and imprisoned and tortured thousands of dissidents. Others, including actress and activist Melina Mercouri, were exiled.

In 1973 students began striking in protest. On 14 November students at Athens Polytechnic – the university immediately south of the archaeological museum – began a sit-in, broadcasting a call for an uprising over their pirate radio station. Three days later, the military sent a tank crashing in. No university students died, but scores of others (the number is still disputed, anywhere from 24 to 40) were killed at companion protests, and hundreds injured.

In the backlash, token 'liberalisation' was halted and an even-harder-line general staged a second coup. But in 1974 the dictatorship collapsed in chaos after Turkey invaded Cyprus. Behind the university's front gates (now forever locked against the military), a large bronze head stands as a memorial to those killed.

The Killing of Alexis Grigoropoulos

In 2008 15-year-old Alexis Grigoropoulos was shot dead by police in Exarhia. The police claimed the teen was an anarchist troublemaker, but eyewitnesses said the kid – who was from a rich suburb of Athens – had only been hanging out with friends.

Greeks were already angry, as Greece's debt crisis was just coming to light, and the conservative government had pushed through unpopular pension cuts and privatisation. Hours after Grigoropoulos's death, Exarhia was teeming with rioters. Demonstrations spread across the country and lasted the rest of the month. Unfortunately this did nothing to halt any of the cutbacks.

Exarhia commemorates the Athens Polytechnic uprising (November 17, now a national holiday) and Grigoropoulos's death (December 6) with chaotic demonstrations. It's wise to steer clear these days; tear gas isn't uncommon.

Athens University   UNIVERSITY

3 ⊙ MAP P136, D4

The splendid Athens University building was designed by the Danish architect Christian Hansen and completed in 1864. Although the university has expanded massively around the city (enrolment is more than 100,000 students), Hansen's building still serves as the university's administrative headquarters and ceremonial hall.

Adjacent to the south is the more ornate Athens Academy, modelled on Plato's Academy and still Greece's most prestigious research institution. The building was designed by Theophil Hansen (brother of Christian) and completed in 1885. The Ionian-style entrance mimics the eastern entrance to the Erechtheion, the temple on the north side of the Acropolis. Admire the two school buildings' neoclassical facades from the street; neither is open to the public. (Panepistimiou 30, Panepistimio; ⊙closed to public; Ⓜ Panepistimio)

Eating

■ Kriti   CRETAN €€

4 ⊗ MAP P136, C3

There is no shortage of Cretan restaurants in Athens, but this is the one that Cretans themselves recommend, especially for rare seasonal treats such as stewed snails, bittersweet pickled *volvi* (wild bulbs) and tender baby goat with nuts and garlic. It occupies

several storefronts inside the arcade; on weekends it's a good idea to reserve. (☎210 382 6998; Veranzerou 5, Omonia; mains €7-12; ⊙noon-midnight Mon-Sat; Ⓜ Omonia)

Yiantes   TAVERNA €€

5 ⊗ MAP P136, E2

This lovely garden restaurant is upmarket for Exarhia, but the food is superb and made with largely organic produce. Expect interesting seasonal greens such as *almirikia* (sea beans), perfectly grilled fish or delicious mussels and calamari with saffron. (☎210 330 1369; Valtetsiou 44, Exarhia; mains €10-18; ⊙1pm-midnight; 🥢; Ⓜ Omonia)

Hypovrihio   GREEK €

6 ⊗ MAP P136, E3

The 'Submarine' is a typical Exarhia hang-out, colourful and cramped. Raki is encouraged, but the booze is offset by a big range of home-cooked Greek standards (pork chops, Cretan rusk salads, lots of veg options) and pastas that meet Italian standards of toothiness. Food comes in 'small' portions, great for solo diners or tasting a range of things. (☎210 409 0058; Asklipiou 53, cnr Arahovis, Exarhia; small plates €4-10; ⊙4pm-4am Sun-Fri, noon-4pm Sun; Ⓜ Panepistimio)

Kimatothrafstis   TAVERNA €

7 ⊗ MAP P136, E3

This great-value, bright and casual little cafe dishes out a range of

Traditional Greek dinner meze table

home-style Greek cooking and alternative fare. Choose from the day's offerings at the cafeteria-style display. Plates come in two sizes: big or small. (☑213 030 8274; Harilaou Trikoupi 49, Exarhia; small/large plate €4/7; ⏰8am-11pm, closed dinner Sun; 🛜🍴; Ⓜ Omonia)

Ama Laxei stis Nefelis GREEK €

8 ❌ MAP P136, E1

This modern *mezedhopoleio* (restaurant specialising in mezedhes) is a minor hike up Exarhia's hill, but you're rewarded with a lovely setting – an old school building, with tables outside in the vine-shaded playground – and super-savoury small plates that go well with drinks. Think pickled octopus and meatballs flavoured with ouzo. (☑210 384 5978; Kalidromiou 49,

Exarhia; mezedhes €5-11; ⏰1pm-12.30am Wed-Sun, from 7pm Mon; 🚌2, 5, 9, 11 to Polytechneio)

Doureios Ippos TAVERNA €

9 ❌ MAP P136, D2

In summer this family-run taverna can look abandoned – but that's because everyone is up on the roof terrace, shaded by the climbing vines. It's been in business since 1965, relatively unchanged, and cooks all its meat over a charcoal fire. (☑210 383 2006; Koletti 21, Exarhia; mains €8-10; ⏰7pm-2am Tue-Sun; Ⓜ Omonia)

Barbagiannis TAVERNA €

10 ❌ MAP P136, E2

An Exarhia institution, this low-key *mayirio* (cookhouse) is popular with students and anyone with a taste for good-value, home-style Greek food. (📞 210 330 0185; Emmanuel Benaki 94, Exarhia; mains €5-8; 🕑lunch & dinner; Ⓜ Omonia)

Hayat TURKISH €

11 🍴 MAP P136, F3

Hayat's Kurdish eats are hearty and well spiced, from the deceptively simple lentil soup to good-value kebab and stews, all served with good chewy bread. Also good for quick snacks. (📞 215 555 8580; Ippokratous 78, Exarhia; mains €4-9; 🕑2pm-midnight; Ⓜ Panepistimio)

Rozalia TAVERNA €

12 🍴 MAP P136, D2

An Exarhia favourite on a lively pedestrian strip, this family-run taverna serves grills and home-style fare. Mezedhes are brought around on a tray, so you can point and pick. Pavement tables are tempting, but better to sit in the garden where the ground is level. (📞 210 330 2933; www.rozalia.gr; Valtetsiou 58, Exarhia; mains €5-11; 🕑noon-2am; Ⓜ Omonia)

Drinking

Nabokov BAR

13 🍷 MAP P136, E3

Just what you expect in an Exarhia bar: literary leanings, retro music, a bit of food and customers who treat it like their life-long haunt, even though it only opened in 2017. There's even a little pinball.

Daytime especially, it's a nice mix of ages. (📞 211 111 0432; Asklipiou 41, Exarhia; 🕑10am-2am Mon-Thu, to 3am Fri & Sat, 6pm-2am Sun; Ⓜ Panepistimio)

Veneti CAFE

14 ☕ MAP P136, B3

Legendary cafe Neon, famous haunt of Athens literati, fell victim to the crisis. But the cavernous space got a decent tenant in Veneti (aka Beneth, if you read the letters in English), which has filled the lower level with good-quality pastries, cookies, pies and even hot meals. There's seating upstairs and out on the square. Excellent service. (📞 210 523 0740; Plateia Omonias 7, Omonia; 🕑7am-11pm; Ⓜ Omonia)

Taf Coffee COFFEE

15 ☕ MAP P136, C3

One of the best of Athens' new wave of coffee roasters, with distribution around the country and a bit abroad. Sip a pour-over here, or grab a quick espresso at the front bar. (📞 210 380 0014; www.cafetaf.gr; Emmanuel Benaki 7, Omonia; 🕑7am-8pm Mon-Fri, 8am-5pm Sat; Ⓜ Omonia)

Ivi COFFEE

16 ☕ MAP P136, D2

There are plenty of options for a freddo espresso right around Exarhia's main square, but this place is extra-pleasant due to its breezy open front and its chill

Exarhia's Sundown Spot

Climb any hill in Greece, and there's usually a cafe. The one on Strefi Hill, **Exostrefis** (☏ 215 551 5656; Logos Strefi, Exarhia; ⏱ 1pm-3am Mon-Fri, 5pm-3am Sat, noon-3pm Sun; 🚌 2, 5, 11 to Polytechnio, 230 to Kallidromio), is a casual place for a coffee or afternoon beer and small snacks, alongside neighbourhood regulars who come up to enjoy the sunset. There's live music weekend evenings (minimum charge €10). In winter, the 'downstairs' location – a restaurant in a basement on Plateia Exarhion – is livelier.

music. It attracts local creatives working on laptops and brainstorming together. (☏ 215 510 0787; Stournari 2, Exarhia; ⏱ 8am-1am; 🛜; Ⓜ Omonia)

Revolt

BAR

17 Ⓗ MAP P136, D2

This small, simple bar with tables spilling out on to a pedestrian street anchors a few solid blocks of good nightlife. The vibrant murals out front are super. Start here and explore down Koletti as far as Mesolongiou, and the pedestrian blocks there. (☏ 210 380 0016; Koletti 29, Exarhia; ⏱ 10am-2am, to 3am Fri & Sat; Ⓜ Omonia)

Tsin Tsin

COCKTAIL BAR

18 Ⓗ MAP P136, D3

Teeny, tiny and a bit out of the way on a little lane. The bartender knows the craft and the loungey feel is relaxing. (☏ 210 384 1460; Kiafas 6, Exarhia; ⏱ 7pm-late; Ⓜ Omonia)

Blue Fox

BAR

19 Ⓗ MAP P136, F3

Athens supports a small but lively swing and rockabilly scene, and Blue Fox, with its big wooden dance floor, is one of its hubs. Weekend nights, you'll likely spot it from the Vespas parked outside. (☏ 6942487225; Asklipiou 91, Exarhia; ⏱ 9pm-2am Thu, to 3am Fri & Sat; Ⓜ Panepistimio)

Tralala

BAR

20 Ⓗ MAP P136, E3

Actors frequent cool Tralala, with its original artwork, lively owners and gregarious atmosphere. (☏ 210 362 8066; Asklipiou 45, Exarhia; ⏱ noon-3am; Ⓜ Panepistimio, Omonia)

Steki Metanaston

CAFE

21 Ⓗ MAP P136, D1

More than a cafe, this is a social centre for migrants and refugees, set in a larger Exarhia squat. The program is varied, and so is the food. Some newly arrived people have used it as a place to cook food from their own countries, so who knows what you'll taste? (www.facebook.com/stekimetanaston; Tsamadou 13a, Exarhia; ☺late morning–midnight; Ⓜ Polytehnion)

Alexandrino
COCKTAIL BAR

22 🍸 MAP P136, E2

This bar feels like a cute tiny French bistro, with excellent wines and cocktails. (📞 210 382 7780; Emmanuel Benaki 69, Exarhia; ☺7pm-late; Ⓜ Omonia)

Entertainment

Feidiou 2 Music Cafe
LIVE MUSIC

23 ⭐ MAP P136, D4

Traditional music, usually *rembetika* (blues songs) and other heartfelt tunes, starts around 10pm most nights at this cosy little space on the edge of Exarhia. Attracts a nice mixed crowd of all ages. (📞 210 330 0060; www.facebook.com/Feidiou2; Fidiou 2, Exarhia; ☺8am-2.30am; Ⓜ Omonia)

National Theatre
THEATRE

24 ⭐ MAP P136, A3

One of the city's finest neoclassical buildings hosts contemporary theatre and ancient plays. The organisation also supports performances in other venues around town and, in summer, in ancient theatres across Greece. Happily for tourists, some of the productions are surtitled in English, and tickets are reasonably priced. (📞 210 528 8100; www.n-t.gr; Agiou Konstantinou 22-24, Omonia; Ⓜ Omonia)

Riviera
CINEMA

25 ⭐ MAP P136, E2

Screening since 1969, the outdoor cinema Riviera tends toward art-house programming, with new indie films and occasional programs of artists' shorts and other one-offs. (📞 210 384 4827; www.facebook.com/riviera.athens; Valtetsiou 46, Exarhia; adult/child €7/6, Wed €5; ☺Jun-Sep; Ⓜ Omonia)

Rembetika Revival

○ Athens' thriving music scene includes a powerful resurgence in *rembetika* (bluesy songs from the early 20th century), and Exarhia is a great place to sample this soulful musical style.

○ One of Athens' longest-running *rembetika* haunts is **Kavouras** (Map p136, D2; 📞 210 381 0202; Themistokleous 64, Exarhia; ☺11pm-late Fri & Sat Sep-Jun; Ⓜ Omonia), where the party goes till dawn (winters only, though; in general, indoor-only venues close in summer).

○ Also check smaller bars in the neighbourhood, on Emmanuel Benaki and an especially lively strip, very popular with students, around the intersection of Koletti and Mesolongiou.

Alexandrino cocktail bar (p143)

Vox   CINEMA

26 ⭐ MAP P136, E2

Vox open-air cinema on Exarhia's main square has been around since 1938, and fortunately has received historic-building designation. Still, it has the rough-and-ready vibe you'd expect in this neighbourhood. Arrive early and have a drink at the ground-floor squat cafe. (📞 210 331 0170; www.facebook.com/vox.athens; Themistokleous 82, Exarhia; adult/child €7/6, Tue €5; Ⓜ Omonia)

AN Club   LIVE MUSIC

27 ⭐ MAP P136, D2

A small spot with a long history of live rock, for lesser-known international and local bands, especially metal. (📞 210 330 5056; www.anclub.gr; Solomou 13-15, Exarhia; Ⓜ Omonia)

Shopping

Plan 59   MUSIC

28 🔒 MAP P136, E2

Between this and Old School next door, your vintage vinyl needs are covered. Both stock a lot of jazz and psychedelia, while Plan 59 has more Greek music as well as books and magazines. (📞 210 384 0589; http://plan59.wordpress.com; Zoodohou Pigis 59, Exarhia; ⏱ 11am-4pm Mon, Wed & Fri, to 8pm Tue & Thu, 11am-5pm Sat; Ⓜ Omonia)

Zacharias   FASHION & ACCESSORIES

29 🔒 MAP P136, E2

A Greek-Spanish duo specialise in silkscreen designs inspired by classical motifs. Especially nice are their leather notebooks, wallets and more, where black ink on the natural hide echoes the colours of Ancient pottery. Some of their work shows up in museum shops, but this storefront and workspace has the best selection. (www.zacharias.es; Zoodohou Pigis 55, Exarhia; ⊙10am-5pm Mon-Sat; MOmonia)

Politeia   BOOKS

30 🏠 MAP P136, D4

Large bookstore that occupies four storefronts. While it doesn't have a dedicated English section, it does stock English-language books, filed in the relevant sections. And because it's on the edge of Exarhia, it's brimming with political theory. (✆210 360 0235; www.politeianet.gr; Asklipiou 1-3, Panepistimio; ⊙9am-9pm Mon-Fri, to 8pm Sat; MPanepistimio)

Loumidi   COFFEE

31 🏠 MAP P136, B3

The Loumidis family built Greece's famous Papagalo coffee brand, now owned by an international conglomerate. The original shop lives on, however, a pretty little jewel-box version of the typical nuts-candy-coffee-booze store that's a cornerstone of every

Athens neighbourhood. (✆210 321 4426; Eolou 106, Omonia; ⊙8am-8pm Mon-Fri, 8am-4pm Sat; MOmonia)

Comicon Shop   COMICS

32 🏠 MAP P136, D2

Browse a full range of Greek indie comics, graphic novels and zines. Conveniently, there's another comics shop across the street too. (✆213 008 0255; www.comicon-shop.gr; Solonos 128, Exarhia; ⊙9am-8.30pm Mon-Fri, to 3.30pm Sat; MOmonia)

Ellinika Kouloudia   FOOD & DRINKS

33 🏠 MAP P136, E2

Right in the thick of Saturday's lively street market, this quaint deli has a delectable array of traditional products, such as honey, cheese and herbs, as well as organic wine and ouzo. (✆210 330 0384; Kalidromiou 51a, Exarhia; ⊙9am-6pm Mon & Wed, 9am-9pm Tue, Thu & Fri, 8am-4pm Sat; MOmonia)

Travel Bookstore   BOOKS

34 🏠 MAP P136, D4

Good central place for maps and guides. (✆210 361 6943; www.travelbookstore.gr; Solonos 71, Panepistimio; ⊙8.30am-4.30pm Mon, Wed & Sat, to 8.30pm Tue, Thu & Fri; MPanepistimio)

Explore ⊛

Filopappou Hill, Thisio & Petralona

This area is all about escaping from the more hectic parts of Athens, whether by chilling out at a quiet cafe or taking a stroll and suddenly finding yourself alone with nothing but lizards and ancient stones. Filopappou and neighbouring hills offer welcome green space, and the neighbourhoods of Thisio and Petralona are a short walk but a world away from the tourist drag.

Filopappou Hill is a natural sundown destination. But if you come in the morning, you may find the wonderful Byzantine Church of Agios Dimitrios Loumbardiaris (p149) open, and you'll have more light and time to appreciate the landscape, and walk over to the adjacent Hill of the Pnyx (p151), and on to the Church of Agia Marina Thission (p151). Urban explorers can wander in Ano (upper) Petralona, and its main street of Troon – or take a break in Thisio's nearby cafe zone. After dark, catch the show at Dora Stratou Dance Theatre (p155) or a film at Thission (p154).

Getting There & Around

Ⓜ Thissio station (green line) and walk up pedestrianised Apostolou Pavlou.

Ⓜ Akropoli station (red line) and walk west on Dionysiou Areopagitou.

Ⓜ Petralona (green line) looks convenient, but due to the hill it can be easier to walk from Thisio.

Neighbourhood Map on p150

Church of Agia Marina Thission (p151) K_SAMURKAS/SHUTTERSTOCK ©

Top Experience
Stroll up Filopappou Hill

*Also called the Hill of the Muses, Filopappou Hill –
along with the Hills of the Pnyx (p151) and Nymph
– was, according to Plutarch, where Theseus
and the Amazons did battle. Today the pine-clad
slopes are a relaxing place for a stroll, plus an
excellent vantage point for photographing the
Acropolis. There are also a few notable ruins.*

⊙ MAP P150, D6

Ⓜ Akropoli

Church of Agios Dimitrios Loumbardiaris

At the foot of Filopappou Hill, this 16th-century **church** (Map p150, D5; M Thissio, Akropoli) may not be the oldest in Athens, but it is certainly one of the loveliest, with a heavy timber roof, marble floors and a permanent scent of incense. A great 1732 fresco of St Dimitrios, astride his horse in a pose copied from ancient images of Alexander the Great, adorns the interior. The churchyard, with its wooden gate and bells, conjures Japan – a touch by modernist architect Dimitris Pikionis.

Socrates' Prison

Enter the cover of pines, with doves cooing, and follow the path to this warren of rooms carved into bedrock. It's said to have been the place Socrates was imprisoned prior to his trial in 399 BCE. During WWII artefacts from the Acropolis and National Archaeological Museum were hidden here, to protect them from Nazi looting.

Shrine of the Muses & Fortifications

Up the marble-cobbled stairs – another work by architect Pikionis, each stone placed just so – you reach a niche in the bedrock, a shrine dedicated to the goddesses of creative inspiration. Even today, grateful or hopeful artists place offerings on a small stone cairn. Also, ruins of 4th and 5th century BCE defensive walls criss-cross the hill.

Monument of Filopappos

The 12m-high marble monument (pictured left) marks the summit of the hill. It was built between CE 114 and 116 in honour of Julius Antiochus Filopappos, a Roman consul and administrator. The top middle niche depicts Filopappos enthroned, the bottom frieze shows him in a chariot with his entourage.

★ Top Tips

o Small paths weave all over the hill, but the paved path to the top starts near the *periptero* (kiosk) on Dionysiou Areopagitou.

o The summit gives one of the best views of the Acropolis and Attica – sunset and evening offer spectacular light.

o The hilltop above the treeline is exposed: bring sunscreen, a hat and water, and rain gear on wet days.

o English-language placards placed at major features explain the rich ancient history of the hill.

✗ Take a Break

For refreshment, drop down to the cafes in Thisio, either on the main pedestrian route or back on Iraklidon; Akropol (p154) is pleasant and homey. Or have a full meal at a restaurant such as Gevomai kai Magevomai (p153).

For reviews see

Sights

Hill of the Pnyx PARK

1 ⦿ MAP P150, D4

North of Filopappou Hill (p148), this hill was the official meeting place of the Democratic Assembly in the 5th century BCE – really, the first site of democracy. You can see the speakers' steps, where the great orators Aristides, Demosthenes, Pericles and Themistocles addressed assemblies. (More recently, politicians have used it for photo ops.) The hill is often empty, save for birds, and its view of the Acropolis' front steps gives a real sense of the temples' centrality to ancient Athenian life. To the northwest is the Hill of the Nymphs, topped with the old Athens observatory, built in 1842. (Ⓜ Thisio)

Herakleidon Museum MUSEUM

2 ⦿ MAP P150, D3

This eclectic private museum examines the interrelation of art, mathematics and philosophy, explored through rotating exhibits on such diverse subjects as ancient Chinese technology and shipbuilding. Around the corner in a restored mansion at Iraklidon 16 there is also a kid-oriented permanent science exhibit, though this is open only on Sundays. The museum also holds one of the world's biggest collections of MC Escher artworks (though it is not always on view). (☏ 210 346 1981; www.herakleidon-art.gr; Apostolou Pavlou 37, Thisio; adult/child €7/free; ⏱ 10am-6pm Wed-Sun; Ⓜ Thisio)

Church of Agia Marina Thission CHURCH

3 ⦿ MAP P150, D3

Striped like a multilayered cake and bursting with red-tile domes, this 1931 church perches on the northwest side of the Hill of the Nymphs. Its murals, with a whiff of art nouveau, are lovely, but the real attraction is the much smaller chapel in the southeast corner, carved directly into the bedrock. It dates to the 11th or 12th century and has long been a site for health and fertility rituals. (Plateia Agias Marinas, Thisio; Ⓜ Thisio)

Bernier/Eliades GALLERY

4 ⦿ MAP P150, C2

This well-established gallery in a grand old home showcases prominent Greek artists and an impressive list of international artists,

Country in the City

In Ano Petralona, on Kallisthenous around Aristragora, the street is lined with small, village-style stone cottages. They were built in the mid-20th century as workers' housing by the architect Dimitris Pikionis, who also designed the paths on Filopappou Hill.

from abstract American impressionists to British pop. (📞 210 341 3935; www.bernier-eliades.gr; Eptachalkou 11, Thisio; 🕑10.30am-6.30pm Tue-Fri, noon-4pm Sat; Ⓜ Thisio)

Melina Merkouri Cultural Centre   MUSEUM

5 ◎ MAP P150, B2

For anyone who loves the Greek tradition of *karagiozis* (shadow puppets), this free museum is a treat, packed with the creations of master puppeteer Haridimos (Sotiris Haritos). There's very little English signage, but the displays tell their own stories. Upstairs is a mock street scene of 'old Athens,' with shop windows of the typesetter, the photo studio, the barber and more. Sundays at 11am there's

a puppet show. (📞 210 345 2150; Irakleidon 66, Thisio; admission free; 🕑10am-8pm Tue-Sat, 10am-2pm Sun; Ⓜ Thisio)

Eating

Steki tou Ilia   TAVERNA €

6 ✗ MAP P150, D2

If there's a line to dine at this no-frills *psistaria* (restaurant serving grilled food), it's worth joining. The payoff is succulent lamb and pork chops, barrel wine and simple dips, chips and salads. In summer, the operation moves across the street into a hidden garden over the train tracks. (📞 210 345 8052; Eptahalkou 5, Thisio; chops per portion/kg €9/30; 🕑noon-1am, to 7pm Sun; Ⓜ Thisio)

Ancient seats on the Hill of the Pnyx (p151)

Early Greek Philosophers

Late-5th and early-4th-century-BCE philosophers introduced new modes of thought rooted in rationality, logic and reason: gifts that have shaped Western philosophy ever since. These are the big names:

Socrates (469–399 BCE) Athens' most noble citizen taught his students to reason for themselves by asking probing questions. He was charged with corrupting the city's youth, then jailed (on Filopappou Hill, according to legend) and sentenced to death by drinking hemlock. His legacy is a mode of reason based on eliminating hypotheses through questions – the so-called Socratic method.

Plato (427–347 BCE) Socrates' star student documented his teacher's thoughts in books such as the *Symposium*. Plato wrote *The Republic* to warn Athens that unless its people respected law and leadership, and educated its youth, it would be doomed.

Aristotle (384–322 BCE) Plato's student established his own school (p107) and worked in fields such as astronomy, physics, zoology, ethics and politics. Aristotle was also the personal physician to Philip II, King of Macedon, and tutor of Alexander the Great.

Oikonomou
TAVERNA €€

7 MAP P150, B5

As typical, no-frills neighbourhood tavernas are slowly disappearing, it's worth making a trip to this stalwart, which excels in home-style stews, cooked with care. (It's also a good reason to visit this nice neighbourhood.) The best way to decide what to eat is to visit the kitchen and peek in the day's array of pots. (210 346 7555; Troon 41, Ano Petralona; mains €8-12; 3pm-10pm Tue-Sat; M Petralona)

Gevomai kai Magevomai
TAVERNA €€

8 MAP P150, D3

Stroll off the pedestrian way to find this small corner taverna with marble-topped tables. Neighbourhood denizens know it as one of the best for home-cooked, simple food with fresh ingredients – a boon in this high-tourist-traffic area. (210 345 2802; Nileos 11, Thisio; mains €6-14; lunch & dinner Tue-Sun; ; M Thisio)

Local Hangouts

o Feeling pup-deprived on vacation? Visit Filopappou and Pnyx in the evening, when residents are out walking their dogs.

o Petralona's *laïki agora* (produce market) takes place on Fridays on Kallisthenous.

Drinking

Upopa Epops   BAR

9 🚌 MAP P150, A3

This bar-restaurant is one of the reasons Petralona is considered a just-the-right-amount-of-cool neighbourhood. It has numerous rooms filled with vintage furniture

and a pretty courtyard, the food and drinks are great and there's often a DJ, but there's always a place to have a conversation. And the name? Latin for the hoopoe bird. (📞212 105 5214; Alkminis 7, Petralona; ⏰10am-2am, to 3am Fri & Sat; Ⓜ Petralona)

Akropol   CAFE

10 🚌 MAP P150, D3

This 'vintage cafe' opened in 2017 but has put a lot of effort into looking and feeling like it's been around for decades, with thoughtful staff and occasional music nights that draw neighbours as well as curious tourists. It's in a prime spot on the pedestrian promenade. (📞210 346 5543; Akamandos 2; ⏰9am-2am; Ⓜ Thisio)

Sin Athina   CAFE

11 🚌 MAP P150, D3

Location, location, location! This cafe-bar sits at the junction of the two pedestrianised cafe strips and has a sweeping view up to the Acropolis. The real magic is on the rooftop – though the menu here is more elaborate and slightly higher-priced. (📞210 345 5550; www.sinathina.gr; Iraklidon 2, Thisio; ⏰8am-late; Ⓜ Thisio)

Entertainment

Thission   CINEMA

12 ⭐ MAP P150, D4

Across from the Acropolis, this is a lovely old-style outdoor cinema in a garden setting. Sit towards the back if you want to catch a glimpse

Iraklidon street

Thission cinema

of the glowing edifice. (📞210 342
0864; www.cine-thisio.gr; Apostolou
Pavlou 7, Thisio; €8; ⏱May-Oct;
Ⓜ Thisio)

Zefiros
CINEMA

13 ⭐ MAP P150, B5

The cinephile's outdoor cinema,
running obscure international
films (sometimes a tricky
subtitle situation) and black-
and-white favourites. (📞210 346
2677; www.facebook.com/zefiros
newstarartcinema; Troon 36, Ano
Petralona; €7, Wed €5; ⏱May-Oct;
Ⓜ Petralona)

Dora Stratou
Dance Theatre
DANCE

14 ⭐ MAP P150, C6

Every summer this company
performs Greek folk dances, showing off the rich variety of regional
costume and musical traditions, at
its open-air theatre on the western
side of Filopappou Hill. It also runs
folk-dancing workshops in summer. (📞210 921 4650; www.grdance.
org; Filopappou Hill; adult/child €15/5;
⏱performances 9.30pm Wed-Fri,
8.30pm Sat & Sun late May-Sep;
Ⓜ Petralona, Akropoli)

Explore ◈

Gazi, Keramikos & Metaxourgio

Gazi's is a typical urban tale: abandoned industrial district is revived by artists and bar owners. A decade passes, the edge becomes the centre, and the transformation continues nearby. Today Keramikos and Metaxourgio, east of Gazi, are where scruffy-cool bars and cafes are popping up, alongside derelict mansions, moped dealerships and Chinese wholesalers.

Before the sun is high, visit the archaeological site of Keramikos (p158), then on to the two Benaki outposts: the Museum of Islamic Art (p163) and 138 Pireos St (p163). (Plan ahead; they have limited hours.) For a break afterwards, it's better to cross the road to Petralona, as central Gazi is a ghost town by day. In the evening, grab dinner at Kanella (p166), then head for multipurpose spaces like Bios (p169), Gazarte (p167) and Treno sto Rouf (p168). In general, the scene is rowdier west of Iera Odos, and quieter to the east. But even if you're not into high-volume Gazi, it's fun to at least stroll through the main square, where people meet to preen and plan their night.

Getting There & Around

Ⓜ Kerameikos (blue line) pops up in the centre of the Gazi neighbourhood.

Ⓜ Thissio (green line) is actually closer to the Keramikos archaeological site.

🚕 Taxis wait in central Gazi, or you can call one. Night rates ('2' on the metre, 60% higher) kick in after midnight.

Neighbourhood Map on p162

Top Experience 📷
Wander the Ruins at Kerameikos

This lush, tranquil site, uncovered in 1861 during the construction of Pireos St, is named for the potters who settled it around 3000 BCE, then on the clay-rich banks of the Iridanos River. But it's better known as a cemetery, used through the 6th century CE, and, ironically, the vividly carved grave markers give a sense of ancient life.

◎ MAP P162, D3

http://odysseus.culture.gr

Ermou 148, Kerameikos

adult/child incl museum €8/free, with Acropolis combo ticket free

🕑 8am-8pm, reduced hours in low season

Ⓜ Thissio

Archaeological Museum

The small but excellent museum contains remarkable *stelae* (grave markers) and sculptures from the site, such as the amazing 4th-century-BCE **marble bull** from the plot of Dionysos of Kollytos, as well as funerary offerings and ancient toys. Outside, don't miss the lifelike stone mountain dog.

Sacred Gate

This gate, of which only foundations remain, was where pilgrims from Eleusis entered the city during the annual **Eleusian procession**. The gate marked the end of the **Sacred Way**, aka Iera Odos, which is now a wide city street that still follows a straight route west to modern Elefsina.

Dipylon Gate

The once-massive Dipylon Gate was the city's main entrance and where the Panathenaic Procession began. The city's prostitutes also gathered here to offer their services to travellers. From a **platform** outside the gate, Pericles gave his famous speech extolling the virtues of Athens and honouring those who died in the first year of the Peloponnesian Wars. Between the Sacred and Dipylon Gates is the foundation of the **Pompeion**, a dressing room for participants in the Panathenaic Procession.

Street of Tombs

Leading off the Sacred Way to the left as you head away from the city is this avenue reserved for the graves of Athens' elite, while ordinary citizens were buried in the bordering areas. Some surviving *stelae* (grave markers) are now in the on-site museum and the National Archaeological Museum. What you see here are mostly replicas, but look for poignant details such as a *stela* showing a girl with her pet dog.

★ Top Tips

o In the middle of the site, align yourself with Iera Odos, beyond the fence to the northwest – this will help you envision the gates and other buildings around the end of this historic road.

o There is no cafe or shop close by; bring water, or a bottle to refill from the tap by the museum.

o Admission to the site and the museum is included in the Acropolis combo ticket.

✕ Take a Break

The best place for refreshments is in Gazi and its cafes and restaurants: A Little Taste of Home (p166) for lunch, say.

Walking Tour 🚶

A Night Around Gazi

The towering pylons of Gazi's gasworks glow red at night, like a beacon to party people, and the maze of streets just beyond are chock-a-block with restaurants and bars. But as Gazi has grown rowdier and more mainstream, the Keramikos area and Metaxourgio, both further northeast, have developed their own quiet, more alternative-minded bar and restaurant scenes.

Walk Facts

Start Plateia Avdi, Metaxourgio

Finish Plateon and Leonidou, Keramikos

Length 1.8km; one hour

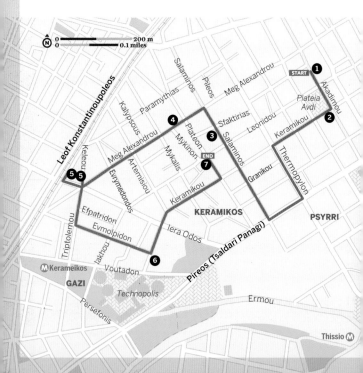

❶ First, a Cocktail

Start your evening on Plateia Avdi, where **Myrovolos** (📞210 522 8806; Giatrakou 12, Metaxourgio; ⏱noon-4am Mon-Fri, 11am-4am Sat & Sun; Ⓜ Metaxourghio) is a funky mixed lesbian-run cafe with an unrelated motorcycle club upstairs – typical Metaxourgio, in other words. There are a few other equally cool cafe-bars on the square as well.

❷ A Trip to the Islands

Seychelles (p165) gets packed every night; if you didn't reserve, scoot in before the 9pm dinner rush. Check the handwritten day's menu of super-fresh regional-Greek dishes, or ask the tattooed chefs in the open kitchen, if they're not too busy. (The story behind the name: it's a joke about the previous business here, a coffee house named Bahamas.)

❸ Edgy Athens

After dinner, wander southeast into Keramikos, and especially the pedestrian street of Salaminos, where **Alphaville** (📞215 505 2001; Salaminos, cnr Sfaktirias, Keramikos; ⏱11am-3am; Ⓜ Thissio, Kerameikos or Metaxourghio) is just one on a strip of near-perfect bohemian bars, all with a good mix of music, inexpensive drinks and loads of *kefi* (party vibes).

❹ Local Blues

Once you've laid on a couple of drinks, see if the band has started at **Steki Pinoklis** (p169), a taverna that usually hosts soulful classic *rembetika* (blues).

❺ Gay Gazi

Gazi has grown into Athens' biggest LGBTIQ+ scene. One of the more recent clubs on the block, **BeQueer** (p167), is super-fun and welcoming, while just around the corner, the city's long-established lesbian club **Noiz** (📞210 346 7850; www.facebook.com/noizclubgaz; Konstantinoupoleos 78, Gazi; ⏱11.30pm-4am Sun, Mon, Wed & Thu, to 6am Fri & Sat; Ⓜ Kerameikos) has retro dance nights.

❻ Hot Jazz

If you're still looking for music, check who's playing at cosy **Afrikana** (p169), a little converted house that crams in jazz and African bands on a stage in the back.

❼ Late-Night Snack

A classic Athens night out ends with souvlaki, even if it's just a skewer or two. **Elvis** (p165) is the hot spot in this area, open after all the bars and almost as raucous.

✗ Street Art

This area rivals Exarhia for excellent graffiti and murals, so you might want to make a separate trip in daytime. Wander on your own, or join a tour with **Alternative Athens** (p20) to learn more about the artists and the themes in their work.

Gazi, Keramikos & Metaxourgio

For reviews see

◎	Top Experiences	p158
◎	Sights	p163
✕	Eating	p165
◎	Drinking	p167
◎	Entertainment	p168

200 m
0.1 miles

Sights

Museum of Islamic Art   MUSEUM

1 MAP P162, E2

While not particularly large, this museum houses one of the world's most significant collections of Islamic art. Four floors of a mansion display, in ascending chronological order, exceptionally beautiful weaving, jewellery, porcelain, even a marble-floored reception room from a 17th-century Cairo mansion. It's all arranged for maximum dazzle, with informative signage. In the basement, part of Athens' ancient Themistoklean wall is exposed, and the top floor has a small cafe with a view of Kerameikos. (210 325 1311; www.benaki.gr; Agion Asomaton 22, Keramikos; adult/student/child €9/7/free; 10am-6pm Thu-Sun; Thissio)

138 Pireos St   MUSEUM

2 MAP P162, B4

While the main Benaki Museum of Greek Culture (p100) displays the Classical and traditional, this annexe focuses on modern and inventive. It hosts only rotating temporary exhibits, so whether you go depends on whether you like what's on at the moment. Also check the schedule of musical performances in its courtyard. It has a pleasant cafe and an excellent gift shop. (Benaki Museum Pireos Annexe; 210 345 3111; www.benaki.gr; Pireos 138, Rouf; €6-8; 11am-9pm Tue-Sun, to 11pm Thu; Kerameikos)

Municipal Gallery of Athens   MUSEUM

3 MAP P162, E1

This city museum shows off Greek artists, primarily from the early and mid-20th century. As the exhibits rotate, the quality varies by what's on, but it's definitely worth a peek – there are always some gems on display. It's set in a grand mansion of many lives, including as the silk factory for which the neighbourhood of Metaxourgio is named. Danish architect Christian Hansen (brother of Theophil, who designed the landmark Athens Academy building on Panepistimiou) designed it in 1833. (210 520 2420; http://odysseus.culture.gr; cnr Leonidou & Millerou, Metaxourgio; admission free; 10am-9pm Tue, to 7pm Wed-Sat, to 4pm Sun; Metaxourghio)

Industrial Gas Museum   NOTABLE BUILDING

4 MAP P162, C3

A walking route runs through the old gasworks in Gazi, a complex of furnaces and industrial buildings from the mid-19th century. The atmosphere is cool, and so are the old photos and film clips. There's a pleasant cafe, and the space is often used for music and other events. (Technopolis; 210 347 5535; www.technopolis-athens.com; Pireos 100, Gazi; adult/child €1/free; 10am-8pm Tue-Sun, to 6pm mid-Oct–mid-Apr; Kerameikos)

Display in the Museum of Islamic Art (p163)

Museum of Traditional Pottery

MUSEUM

5  MAP P162, E3

If the Kerameikos site sparks your curiosity, head to this small museum around the corner. In a lovely neoclassical building, it's dedicated to the history of (relatively) contemporary Greek pottery, exhibiting a selection from the museum's collection of 4500-plus pieces. There's a reconstruction of a traditional potter's workshop. The centre holds periodic exhibitions. (☑210 331 8491; www.potterymuseum.gr; Melidoni 4-6, Keramikos; admission free; ⊙9am-3pm Mon-Fri Sep-Jul; M Thissio)

Hammam

SPA

6  MAP P162, E3

The marble-lined steam room may be a bit small, but thanks to the

attention to detail throughout this Turkish-style bathhouse is the best of the three in central Athens. It has all the amenities you'd find further east, from proper-size water bowls to hot tea in the lounge after. For the full effect, reserve ahead for a full-body scrub. (☑210 323 1073; www.hammam.gr; Melidoni 1, cnr Agion Asomaton, Keramikos; 1hr €25, bath-scrub combos from €45; ⊙12.30-10pm Mon-Fri, 10am-10pm Sat & Sun; M Thissio)

Latraac

SKATING

7  MAP P162, D1

If you ever thought the problem with skateboarding was that there was nowhere to drink a coffee while you did it, the Greeks have solved this for you. A wooden skate bowl occupies one half of a city lot; picnic benches take up the other. The crowd skews adult and arty, but kids are welcome. Food is good too. (www.facebook.com/atraac; Leonidou 63-65, Keramikos; admission free; ⏱skating noon-3pm & 5.30-11pm, cafe to 1am Tue-Sun; Ⓜ Keramikos, Thissio)

Eating

Seychelles
GREEK €€

📵 MAP P162, E1

Gutsy, fresh food, an open kitchen, earnest service, a handwritten daily menu and David Bowie on the soundtrack: Seychelles may be the Platonic ideal of a restaurant. Dishes can look simple – meaty pan-fried mushrooms with just a sliver of sheep's cheese, say, or greens with fish roe – but the

flavour is incomparable. Go early or book ahead; it's deservedly popular. (📞210 118 3478; Kerameikou 49, Metaxourgio; mains €7-16; ⏱10am-3am; Ⓜ Kerameikos)

Elvis
GREEK €

9 🍴 MAP P162, D2

This souvlaki joint is mobbed, and not just because the counter staff slide you a shot of booze while you're waiting. The meat quality is high, the prices are right and the music is great. Every skewer comes with good chewy bread and fried potatoes. (📞210 345 5836; Plataion 29, Keramikos; skewers €1.50; ⏱noon-3am Sun-Thu, noon-5am Fri & Sat; Ⓜ Kerameikos or Thissio)

Greek dish of Chicken Souvlaki

Menu

Advice

○ Restaurants are required to post a menu outside. On long menus, only items with prices are available. When in doubt, order the day's specials.

○ Upscale restaurants automatically bring bottled water, but it's fine to request tap. Bread is technically optional too. Neither is expensive, though.

○ Dishes are typically served (and portioned) to share. Traditional places will usually do half portions for solo diners.

○ Thanks to Orthodox fasting rules, traditional restaurants often have some meat-free and even vegan dishes. Best selection is during Lent, before Christmas and in summer.

○ Frozen ingredients, especially seafood, are usually flagged on the menu with an asterisk.

○ Fish is usually sold per kilogram and cooked whole. It is customary to go into the kitchen to select your fish (go for firm flesh and shiny eyes). Confirm the raw weight so there are no surprises on the bill.

A Little Taste of Home
GREEK €

10 MAP P162, B3

You might expect a restaurant owned by a Syrian refugee to serve Syrian food, but this is solid Greek, plus creative salads – all good and fresh, and indeed, a nice homey place in the middle of party-scene Gazi. Ahmad is an excellent host. (☎210 341 0013; www.alittletaste ofhome.gr; Dekeleon 3, Gazi; mains €8-11; ☯6-11pm Tue-Fri, 7pm-midnight Sat, 2-11pm Sun; ⓂKerameikos)

Kanella
TAVERNA €

11 MAP P162, C2

Housemade village-style bread, mismatched retro crockery and brown paper on the tabletops set the tone for this modern taverna serving regional Greek cuisine. Friendly staff serve daily specials such as lemon lamb with potatoes, and an excellent zucchini and avocado salad. (☎210 347 6320; www.kanellagazi.gr; Leoforos Konstantinoupoleos 70, Gazi; dishes €7-11; ☯1pm-2am, to 3am Fri & Sat; ⓂKerameikos)

Oinomperdemata
TAVERNA €

12 MAP P162, B4

Unpretentious, fresh daily specials are the hallmark of this simple spot with the hip converted-grocery-store look. Try staples such as fried cod with garlic dip and roast vegetables, or pork stew, rabbit and rooster. (📞210 341 1461; www.oinomperdemata.gr; Vasiliou tou Megalou 10, Gazi; mains €5-10; 🕐noon-12.30am Mon-Sat; 📶; Ⓜ Kerameikos)

Aleria

MEDITERRANEAN €€€

13 🍴 MAP P162, D1

This contemporary, elegant restaurant in a restored mansion feels a bit out of place in the otherwise scruffy Metaxourgio neighbourhood. Still, it does lovely things with Greek ingredients. (📞210 522 2633; www.aleria.gr; Megalou Alexandrou 57, Metaxourgio; mains €20-28, set menus from €48; 🕐7.30-11.15pm Mon-Sat, closed late Aug; Ⓜ Metaxourghio)

Drinking

Gazarte

BAR

14 🍺 MAP P162, C2

At this varied arts complex, you'll find a cinema-sized screen playing videos, amazing city views taking in the Acropolis, mainstream music and a trendy 30-something crowd. A ground-level theatre hosts music and comedy. There's occasional live music and a restaurant to boot. (📞210 346 0347; www.gazarte.gr; Voutadon 32-34, Gazi; Ⓜ Kerameikos)

BeQueer

LGBTIQ+

15 🍺 MAP P162, C2

Gazi's gay scene can be a little homogenous and high-style, so this quirkier, more casual club was

Technopolis (p169)

welcomed warmly when it opened in late 2017. The vibe is friendly and open, and there are occasional theme and drag nights. (☏ 213 012 2249; Keleou 10, Gazi; ⏱ 11.45pm-6am Fri & Sat; Ⓜ Kerameikos)

Laika

BAR

16 📍 MAP P162, C1

Out on the fringes of Gazi, amid car workshops and the occasional experimental theatre, this hip little cafe-bar is a treat. There's a good food menu, and often music at night. (☏ 215 501 3801; Pellis 30, Votanikos; ⏱ noon-2am Tue-Sun; Ⓜ Kerameikos)

Beaver Collective

CAFE

17 📍 MAP P162, A4

This all-women-run cooperative cafe is of course lesbian-friendly, but also just generally friendly. Brunch gets a good crowd and cocktails flow freely. (☏ 211 210 3540; Vasiliou tou Megalou 46, Rouf; ⏱ 1.30pm-2am, 5.30pm-2am Sun; Ⓜ Kerameikos)

Big

LGBTIQ+

18 📍 MAP P162, B1

Cosy hub for Athens' lively bear scene. (☏ 6946282845; Falesias 12, Votanikos; ⏱ 10pm-3am Tue-Thu & Sun, to 5am Fri & Sat; Ⓜ Kerameikos)

A Liar Man

BAR

19 📍 MAP P162, C2

A tiny hideout with a more hushed vibe – a nice antidote to other top-volume bars and clubs nearby. It

closes in summer. (☏ 210 342 6322; www.facebook.com/aliarmanathens; Sofroniou 2, Gazi; ⏱ 5pm-2am Mon-Thu, to 4am Fri & Sat, 2pm-1am Sun mid-Sep–mid-Jun; Ⓜ Kerameikos)

S-Cape

LGBTIQ+

20 📍 MAP P162, C3

Stays packed with the younger gay, lesbian and transgender crowd. Check theme nights online. (Iakhou 32, Gazi; ⏱ 11.30pm-5am; Ⓜ Kerameikos)

MoMix

COCKTAIL BAR

21 📍 MAP P162, C2

Cocktails get the molecular treatment here, arriving at the table fizzing or smoking, or transformed into gums and powders. Don't be put off by the harsh front room – it opens into a pleasant back garden. (☏ 6974350179; www.momixbar.com; Keleou 1, Gazi; ⏱ 8pm-3am, to 4am Fri & Sat; Ⓜ Kerameikos)

Entertainment

Treno sto Rouf

ARTS CENTRE

22 ⭐ MAP P162, A4

Look for the glowing headlight on a steam locomotive behind Rouf station. Attached is a string of old train cars converted into a restaurant, bar-cafe, music club and theatre. Even when nothing's scheduled, it's a cool place to have a drink and a snack (€6 to €15) and imagine yourself on the Orient Express. (☏ 210 529 8922; www.totrenostorouf.gr; Konstantinoupoleos,

Rouf; ⏰8pm-late Tue-Sat Sep-Jul;
🚊21 or B16 to Rouf, Ⓜ Kerameikos)

Steki Pinoklis   TRADITIONAL MUSIC

23 ⭐ MAP P162, D1

Although this taverna opened
only in 2017, its musical taste and
style skews much older. This is an
excellent place to hear *rembetika*
(blues) songs from Smyrna and
other traditional Greek music,
with a band playing most nights
(starting at 9.30pm or 10pm) and
Sunday afternoons (usually from
4pm). Food is average, but not
expensive. (📞210 577 7355; www.
facebook.com/pinoklis; Megalou Alexandrou 102, Keramikos; ⏰8pm-2am
Wed-Sat, 2-10pm Sun; Ⓜ Kerameikos)

Afrikana   JAZZ

24 ⭐ MAP P162, D2

Just out of the fray of the Gazi
scene, this little bar occupies an
old house, and its small stage
hosts jazz and funk bands almost
every night. The atmosphere is
very friendly and draws a nice
mixed crowd. Cover for the band
is usually €5 or so, added to the
price of your first drink. (📞210 341
0445; www.facebook.com/afrikana.
athens; Ierofonton 13, Gazi; ⏰7.30pm-
2.30am Tue-Sun; Ⓜ Kerameikos)

Bios   LIVE MUSIC, GALLERY

25 ⭐ MAP P162, D2

Occupying a Bauhaus apartment
building, this multilevel warren

Blocks to Avoid

The east end of Metaxourgio
is what gives the neighbourhood its somewhat dodgy
reputation. Better not to stray
into the smaller streets east
of Plateia Avdi, where there's
open-air drug use, as well as
two blocks of lowest-budget
brothels. The pink 'Studio'
neon signs, dotted around Gazi
and Keramikos, mark brothels
as well, of a more upscale sort.

---

has a bar, a basement club, a tiny
art-house cinema and a roof deck.
Expect live performances, art and
new-media exhibitions, or at the
very least a solid DJ and an Acropolis
view. In colder months, most activity
is in Tesla, the ground-floor bar.
(📞210 342 5335; www.bios.gr; Pireos 84,
Keramikos; ⏰11am-late; Ⓜ Thissio)

Technopolis   PERFORMING ARTS

26 ⭐ MAP P162, C3

There's always something on
at the city's old gasworks, the
impressively restored 1862
complex of furnaces and industrial
buildings. It hosts multimedia
exhibitions, concerts, festivals and
special events and has a pleasant cafe. (📞210 346 7322; www.
technopolis-athens.com; Pireos 100,
Gazi; Ⓜ Kerameikos)

Worth A Trip 📷
Faliro

On a baking-hot summer day in central Athens, don't forget that the sea is only 7 kilometres south. An excursion to the waterfront all but guarantees a refreshing breeze, and it's a great opportunity to join Athenian families at leisure, whether along the waterfront promenade or at the Stavros Niarchos Park and adjacent arts centre.

🚋 From Syntagma, destination Faliro. It runs past Flisvos Park and continues to near the Stavros Niarchos Center.

🚌 Faster if going directly to Stavros Niarchos Center.

🚗 A taxi to Flisvos Park costs about €12.

Flisvos Park

The highly family-friendly **Flisvos Park** (pictured; Palaio Faliro; admission free; ⏱24hr; ♿; 🚊Parko Flisvou) has loads of playground facilities, an open-air cinema and the wonderful summer-only shadow-puppet theatre, **Theatro Skion Tasou Konsta** (📞210 322 7507; www. tkt.gr; Flisvos Park, Palaio Faliro; €3.50; ⏱8.30pm Fri-Sun Jun-Sep; ♿; 🚊Park Flisvou). This is a lively place around sundown, as locals come out for a *volta* (stroll) along the promenade.

Stavros Niarchos Foundation Cultural Center

The vast **Stavros Niarchos Foundation Cultural Center** (📞216 809 1001; www.snfcc. org; Leoforos Syngrou 364, Kallithea; admission free; 🚌550 to Onasseio, 10 to Epaminonda) spreads its winged roof on a hill above Faliron Bay. Architecture buffs will love the Renzo Piano building, and readers can admire the National Library installed in one wing. Check the schedule for arts events by the grand pool, and at the **Greek National Opera** (Ethniki Lyriki Skini; 📞210 366 2100; www.nationalopera.gr), also based here.

Stavros Niarchos Park

Athens is short on green spaces, so **Stavros Niarchos Park** (www.snfcc.org; Synggrou 364, Kallithea; admission free; ⏱6am-midnight Apr-Oct, to 8pm Nov-Mar; 🚌550 to Onasseio, 10 to Epaminonda) is a true breath of fresh air. A large central lawn hosts free dance and exercise classes, as well as midnight movie marathons in summer, while rambling paths cut through patches of lavender and rows of olive trees. A playground, interactive sound installations and rental bikes (€1 per hour) add to the fun.

★ Top Tips

o Be sure you're on a Faliro-bound tram, as the line splits near the sea.

o In addition to public transport, the Stavros Niarchos Foundation runs a shuttle bus from Syntagma, several times daily on weekdays and every 30 minutes 9.30am to 11pm on weekends.

o The waterfront along the Faliro tram line is rocky, but some people do swim. Get off the tram at Mousson for the easiest water access.

✕ Take a Break

There are two cafes and a bistro, open till midnight, in Stavros Niarchos Park, and some restaurants and snacks in Flisvos Park. You could also continue to Piraeus for dinner at Michelin-starred **Varoulko** (📞210 522 8400; www.varoulko.gr; Akti Koumoundourou 52, Mikrolimano; mains €45-65; ⏱1pm-1am).

Survival Guide

Parthenon (p35), Acropolis WESTEND61/GETTY IMAGES ©

Before You Go

Book Your Stay

○ Athens offers the full range of options, but rooms can be a bit drab for the price, especially in the midrange.

○ Book two months ahead for best selection; for summer, four months ahead.

○ Pools are scarce, and wi-fi can be sluggish even in high-end places.

Useful Websites

Boutique Athens (www.boutique athens.com) Spacious apartments and whole houses all over town.

Lonely Planet (lonely planet.com/athens/ hotels) More recommendations and bookings.

Best Budget

Phaedra (www. hotelphaedra.com) A family-run gem on a prime corner in Plaka.

Evripides (www.evripid eshotel.gr) Budget travellers deserve rooftop Acropolis-view breakfasts too.

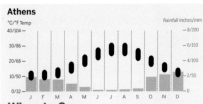

Athens

°C/°F Temp · Rainfall inches/mm

When to Go

Summer (Jun–Aug) Peak heat and prices, but great outdoor festivals and street life. Athenians leave in August; some bars and shops close. (Also applies to Easter.)

Autumn (Sep-Oct) Milder temps, thinner crowds. Accommodation prices usually drop by 20%.

Winter (Nov–Mar) Cooler, with occasional rain or snow. Lively arts and nightlife. Cheapest lodging, but can be chilly.

Spring (Apr–May) Ideal weather, few crowds. Reasonable accommodation, and, in May, outdoor cinemas and restaurants start to open.

City Circus (www.city-circus.gr) Win Instagram with #hostellife pics from this hip spot.

Marble House Pension (www.marblehouse.gr) Wave to the neighbours on the alley.

Best Midrange

InnAthens (www.inn athens.com) Excellent value for such good style and location.

Phidias Hotel (www. phidias.gr) Balcony view on Athens' best pedestrian street.

Lozenge (www.lozenge hotel.com) Quiet and

chic, for a good price in a prime area.

Alice Inn (www. aliceinnathens.com) Just four rooms in this pretty Plaka town house.

Best Top End

Athens Was (www. athenswas.gr) No better location for visiting the Acropolis.

Grande Bretagne (www. grandebretagne.gr) Athens' grande dame.

Electra Palace (www. electrahotels.gr) 'Palace' is well earned.

Accommodation by Neighbourhood

Neighbourhood	For	Against
Plaka	Atmosphere. Close to Acropolis.	Definitely tourist central.
Syntagma	Larger rooms with best amenities.	Big 1970s buildings can be characterless.
Monastiraki & Psyrri	Scenic, easiest metro access from airport.	Noise from bars, open till 4am on weekends.
Acropolis Area	Local vibe in Makrygianni and Koukaki.	Koukaki is a 15-minute walk to the Acropolis.
Kolonaki	Quiet. Convenient to museums.	Long walk or short metro ride to Plaka.
Omonia	Some good new and renovated hotels.	Visible drug use and prostitution at night.
Exarhia	Vibrant nightlife and restaurants.	Few hotels. Far from central sights.
Thisio & Petralona	Pleasant, modern. Very few tourists.	Few hotels, and 10- to 15-minute walk to Acropolis.
Mets & Pangrati	Quiet, with good restaurants.	Only one hotel. Reach Acropolis by bus or 20-minute walk.
Gazi, Keramikos & Metaxourgio	Athens' hipster fringes, with good bars.	Gazi is loud. Eastern end of Metaxourgio is seedy.

Coco-Mat (www.cocomatathens.com) Best design feature: the house-brand beds.

Arriving in Athens

Eleftherios Venizelos International Airport

Athens' **airport** (ATH; ☎ 210 353 0000; www.aia.gr), at Spata, 27km east of Athens, is a manageable single terminal.

Transport Options

Metro Line 3 One-way/return within seven days €10/18, 50 minutes to Monastiraki, every 30 minutes between 6.30am and 11.30pm

Bus X95 €6, one hour to 1½ hours to Sytagma, every 20 to 30 minutes, 24 hours

Taxi Flat fare to centre, tolls included, day/night €38/54, 30 to 45 minutes. Night fare applies to drop-off time, not pickup.

Welcome Pickups (www.welcomepick-ups.com) Book car ahead, at the same flat rate as regular taxis.

Port of Piraeus

⊙ Most island ferries and all cruise ships arrive at **Piraeus** (☎ 210 455 0000, €0.89 per 1min 14541; www.olp.gr), southwest of Athens.

o Free shuttle buses run inside the enormous port zone and stop across the road from the metro.

Greek Ferries (📞 2810 529000; www.greek ferries.gr) Schedules and tickets

Transport Options

Metro Line 1 €1.40, 30 minutes to Thissio, 5.30am to midnight

Bus X80 From the cruise-ship port to major sites, €4, 30 minutes to the Acropolis, May to October only

Bus 040 To Syntagma, €1.40, every 30 minutes, 24 hours

Night bus 500 To Omonia, €1.40, 45 minutes, hourly midnight to 5am

Taxi Drivers waiting in front of the metro are notorious for over-

charging. Hail from the street if possible. Expect to pay €20 to €25, on the meter, to the centre.

Getting Around

Metro

o Three lines: Line 1 (green, to Piraeus), Line 2 (red), Line 3 (blue, to the airport, though some trains end a few stops earlier).

o Maps have clear icons and English labels. All stations have elevators and wheelchair access.

o Trains operate from 5.30am to 12.30am, every four minutes during peak periods and every 10 minutes off-peak. Last airport train

is 11pm. On Friday and Saturday, lines 2 and 3 run till 2.30am.

o Information: www.stasy.gr.

Taxi

o Short trips around central Athens cost about €5.

o Normal tariff is marked '1' on the meter; after midnight and holidays, the tariff is '2', about 60% higher.

o If a taxi picks you up while already carrying passengers, each person pays the fare on the meter minus any diversions to drop others (note what it's at when you get in).

o To the airport, drivers often propose a flat fare of €40, about the same as the meter with all legitimate add-ons (tolls, airport fee, luggage fees).

o For street hailing, thrust your arm out vigorously and shout your destination.

o Taxi apps ease many difficulties: **Beat** (www.thebeat.co/gr), **Taxiplon** (www.taxiplon.gr).

o For day trips, **Athens Tour Taxi** (📞 6932295395; www.athenstourtaxi.com) is recommended.

Transport Options

Walking Central Athens is compact. Likely what you'll do the most.

Metro Fast, efficient, most useful for visitors.

Taxis Affordable. Drivers speak little English.

Buses Go everywhere, but no printed maps.

Tram Slow but scenic way to the coast.

Car Unnecessary and stressful, due to narrow streets and congestion; avoid.

Tickets & Passes

The reloadable paper **Ath.ena Ticket** works on buses, the tram and the metro. Buy from machines or offices in the metro. (A sturdy plastic Ath.ena Card is also available, only from ticket offices.) Ath.ena Tickets issued for express buses (from the airport, for example) cannot be reloaded.

Single ticket (90 minutes, unlimited transfers)	€1.40
24-hour pass	€4.50
Five-day pass	€9
Three-day pass with round-trip airport ticket	€22

Children under six travel free. Under 18 or over 65 are half-fare, but you must buy at a ticket office.

On the metro, tap the card at the turnstiles. On buses and trams, board at any door and tap on the validation machine.

Bus

o Typical service is every 15 minutes, 5am to midnight.

o For directions and routes, use Google Maps or the trip planner at the website of the bus company, **OASA** (www.oasa. gr); click 'Telematics'.

o Useful lines for tourists are electric trolleybuses 2, 5, 11 and 15, from Syntagma to the National Archaeological Museum.

Tram

o The tram line runs from Syntagma, opposite the National Gardens, to the coast, then splits: east to Voula (one hour) and west to Faliro

(45 minutes) and, when an extension opens in 2019, Piraeus.

o Service is from 5.30am to 1am Sunday to Thursday (every 10 minutes), and to 2.30am on Friday and Saturday (every 40 minutes).

o Ticket machines are on the platforms.

o Information: www. stasy.gr

Bicycle

o No cycle lanes, reckless drivers and loads of hills. But some hardy locals do ride, and sightseeing by bike can be efficient (and breezy).

o A bike route runs from Thisio to the coast. Roll

in Athens (p20) leads a very nice tour.

o For bicycle hire, see Funky Ride (p44).

Essential Information

Business Hours

o Some restaurants and bars scale back opening days in winter.

o Live-music bars without outdoor space usually shut for the whole summer.

o Many smaller businesses and shops close for an hour or two in the afternoon.

o As a general rule:

Banks 8.30am–2.30pm Monday to Thursday, 8am–2pm Friday

Cafes 9am–midnight

Bars 6pm–2am or 4am

Clubs 10pm–4am

Restaurants noon–10pm

Shops 8am–3pm Monday, Wednesday and Saturday; 8am–2.30pm & 5–8pm Tuesday, Thursday and Friday

Discount Cards

Athens Spotlighted (www.athenspotlight ed.gr) From the **Athens Airport Information Desk** (⊘24hr). Discounts at select shops, restaurants and a few sights. Free.

European Youth Card (www.eyca.org) Ages 13 to 30. Need not be a resident of Europe. €10.

International Student Identity Card (ISIC; www.isic.org) Students age 12 to 30. €10.

Seniors Card-carrying EU pensioners.

Electricity

Type C
220V/50Hz

Type F
230V/50Hz

Emergencies & Police

Ambulance	☎116
Emergency	☎112
Police	☎100
Tourist Police	☎171

If calling from a non-Greek number, only ☎112 connects.

Central Police Station (☎210 770 5711, emergency 100; www.astynomia.gr; Leoforos Alexandras 173, Ambelokipi; Ⓜ Ambelokipi)

Pangrati Police Station (☎210 725 7000, emergency 100; Mimnermou 6-8; Ⓜ Syntagma) Most convenient for visitors.

Tourist Police Station (☎210 920 0724, 24hr 171; Veïkou 43-45, Koukaki; ⊘8am-10pm; Ⓜ Sygrou-Fix, Akropoli)

Health

Check pharmacy windows for details of the nearest duty pharmacy, or call ☎1434 (Greek only). There's a 24-hour pharmacy at the airport.

SOS Doctors (☎210 821 1888, 1016; www.sosiatroi.gr; ⊘24hr) Pay service with English-speaking doctors who make house/hotel calls.

Dos & Don'ts

Body language 'Yes' is a swing of the head and 'no' is a quick raising of the head or eyebrows, often accompanied by a 'tsk'.

Eating If invited out, do offer to pay, but don't insist. Don't rush dinner or the waitstaff.

Photography In churches, avoid using a flash or photographing the main altar. At archaeological sites, using a tripod marks you as a professional and may require special permission.

Places of worship Cover shoulders and knees. Some churches will deny admission if you're showing too much skin.

Internet Access

○ Most hotels have internet access and wi-fi, though it is not always very fast.

○ Free wireless hot spots are at Syntagma, Thisio, Gazi and the port of Piraeus.

○ **Cosmote** maintains public data hot spots; buy prepaid cards at Cosmote or Germanos stores.

Left Luggage

There is reasonably priced (from €3.50/6hr) storage at the airport, and most hotels store luggage free for guests. Also:

Athens Lockers (☏ 213 035 4760; www.athenslockers.com; Athinas 2; €4-11; �l 8am-9pm May-Oct, to 8pm Apr-Nov; Ⓜ Monastiraki)

LeaveYourLuggage. gr (☏ 211 410 8440; www.leaveyourluggage.gr; Voulis 36; €4-11; �l 8am-9pm May-Oct, to 8pm Nov-Apr; 🛜; Ⓜ Syntagma)

Money

○ Shops and restaurants are required to have card payment systems, but cash is still far more commonly used.

○ Major banks have branches around Syntagma. ATMs are plentiful enough in commercial districts, but harder to find in more residential areas.

National Bank of Greece (☏ 210 334 0500; cnr Karageorgi Servias & Stadiou, Syntagma; Ⓜ Syntagma) Has a 24-hour automated exchange machine.

Onexchange Currency and money transfers. Branches: **Syntagma** (☏ 210 331 2462; www.onexchange.gr; Karageorgi Servias 2, Syntagma; �l 9am-9pm; Ⓜ Syntagma), **Monastiraki** (☏ 210 322 2657; www.onexchange.gr; Areos 1, Monastiraki; �l 9am-9pm; Ⓜ Monastiraki).

Tipping

Hotels and Ferries Bellhops and stewards expect a small gratuity of €1 to €3.

Restaurants If a service charge is included, just round up the bill. If there's no service charge, leave 10% to 20%.

Taxis Round up the fare by a couple of euros. There's a small fee for handling bags; this is an official charge, not a tip.

Post

The Greek postal system is slow. Larger post offices sell boxes for shipping.

Athens Central Post Office (☎ 210 335 3383; www.elta.gr; Eolou 100, Omonia; ⏰7.30am-8.30pm Mon-Fri, to 2.30pm Sat; Ⓜ Omonia)

Public Holidays

All banks and shops and most museums and ancient sites close on these holidays, as well as Orthodox holidays with movable dates.

New Year's Day 1 January

Epiphany 6 January

Greek Independence Day 25 March

Labour Day (Protomagia) 1 May

Feast of the Assumption 15 August

Ohi Day 28 October

Christmas Day 25 December

St Stephen's Day 26 December

Safe Travel

○ During the financial crisis, crime has risen in Athens. But this is a rise from almost zero, and violent street crime remains relatively rare.

○ Stay aware of your surroundings at night, especially in streets southwest of Omonia, where prostitutes and drug users gather.

○ Phone snatching is on the rise. Don't stand on the street absorbed in your phone or leave it on restaurant tables.

○ Pickpockets operate especially on the metro green line (Piraeus–Kifisia), around Omonia and Athinas and at the Monastiraki Flea Market.

○ Scammers target solo male travellers. Be wary of invitations to bars, which can end in exorbitant bills and/or adulterated drinks.

○ It's mandatory to wear a mask in all indoor public places, in all areas of Greece. Proof of vaccination is required to enter indoor public spaces such as restaurants and museums.

○ Strikes

○ Strikes and demonstrations can disrupt public transport and close sights and shops, but they are almost always announced in advance. Demonstrations usually begin or end at Plateia Syntagmatos.

○ Check www.livingingreece.gr/strikes for the latest.

○ Given the frequency of strikes in and around

Greek Orthodox Holidays

These are all official holidays, and many people take the full week preceding Easter as a vacation. Book hotels and travel well in advance.

Year	First Monday in Lent	Good Friday to Easter Monday	Pentecost Monday
2022	7 March	22-25 April	13 June
2023	27 February	14-17 April	5 June
2024	18 March	3-6 May	24 June
2025	3 March	18-21 April	9June

Athens, travel insurance is recommended.

Smoking

An estimated 40% of Greek adults smoke. Smoking in enclosed public places is banned, but this often goes unheeded in bars. Outdoor seating is well used by smokers. Vaping is not very common.

Telephone

○ Greece country code: ☏30.

○ Athens landline numbers begin with ☏21; mobile numbers begin with ☏6.

○ Public phones allow international calls. Purchase cards at kiosks (*periptera*).

○ SIM cards are reasonably priced. Buy at major phone shops. You must show your passport.

○ US/Canadian phones must have a dual- or tri-band system; also make sure your phone is carrier-unlocked.

Toilets

○ Public toilets are rare. If you use a cafe bathroom, it's polite to buy something.

○ Greek plumbing is fragile and does not accommodate toilet paper. It should be placed in the small bin provided next to every toilet.

Tourist Information

Athens Airport Information (⏱24hr) For logistics and Athens Spotlighted discount card.

Athens City Information Acropolis (☏ 210 321 7116; www. thisisathens.org; Dionysiou Areopagitou & Leoforos Syngrou; ⏱9am-9pm mid-May–Sep; Ⓜ Akropoli)

Athens City Information Airport (☏ 210 353 0390; www.thisisathens. org; ⏱8am-8pm; Ⓜ Airport)

EOT (Greek National Tourism Organisation; ☏ 210 331 0716, 210 331 0347; www. visitgreece.gr; Dionysiou Areopagitou 18-20, Makrygianni; ⏱8am-8pm Mon-

Fri, 10am-4pm Sat & Sun May-Sep, 9am-7pm Mon-Fri Oct-Apr; Ⓜ Akropoli) Current site hours and bus and train times. Also at the **airport** (9am to 5pm Monday to Friday and 10am to 4pm Saturday).

Travellers with Disabilities

○ The 2004 Paralympic Games improved accessibility, but marble and stepped alleys are challenging for wheelchairs.

○ Visual and hearing impairments are rarely catered to, but there are tactile sidewalk strips.

○ Download Lonely Planet's free **Accessible Travel** guide from https://shop.lonelyplanet.com/categories/accessible-travel.com.

Matt Barrett's Greece Guides (www.greecetravel.com/handicapped) Local articles, resorts and tour groups.

Sage Traveling (www.sagetraveling.com/athens-accessibletravel) A wheelchair rider's experience.

Visas

Australia, Canada, Israel, Japan, New Zealand and USA No visa required for tourist visits of up to 90 days.

EU No visa required.

UK Starting on January 1, 2023, UK travllers will need an ETIAS visa-waiver to visit Greece. See http://etias.com for more information.

Other countries Check with a Greek embassy or consulate.

Responsible Travel

Overtourism

o Visit September through to April to avoid the summer season peak density of crowds.

o Arrive at the Acropolis as soon as the site opens, or wait until towards the end of the day when crowds have thinned.

o Other superb archaeological sites, such as the Ancient Agora and Kerameikos, can be blissfully quiet first thing in the morning or towards sunset.

o Take advantage of Athens' greens spaces such as Filopappou Hill, Lykavittos Hill, National Gardens, Stavros Niarchos Park and Strefi Hill in Exarhia.

Support local & give back

o Look out for Wise Greece products where a percentage of the profit goes into a fund

to buy food for people in need; you'll find them at the Kypseli Municipal Market (p21).

o Support Shedia, a social and environmental project providing education, training and jobs for homeless and poor people, by dining at their stylish cafe-bar Shedia Home (p73) and buying from their arts and crafts gifts range.

Leave a light footprint

o At your accommodation reuse your bath towels rather than have them changed each day.

o A bike route runs from Thisio to the coast. A few outfits offer bicycle hire, such as Funky Ride (p44) and Solebike (p20).

Language

Greek is believed to be one of the oldest European languages, with an oral tradition of 4000 years and a written tradition of approximately 3000 years.

The Greek alphabet can look a bit intimidating if you're used to the Roman alphabet, but with a bit of practice you'll start recognising the characters quickly. If you read our pronunciation guides as if they were English, you'll be understood. Note that 'm/f/n' indicates masculine, feminine and neuter forms.

To enhance your trip with a phrasebook, visit lonelyplanet. com. Lonely Planet iPhone phrasebooks are available through the Apple App store.

Basics

Hello.
Γειά σας.   ya·sas (polite)
Γειά σου.   ya·su (informal)

Good morning/evening.
Καλή μέρα/   ka·li me·ra/
σπέρα.   spe·ra

Goodbye.
Αντίο.   an·di·o

Yes./No.
Ναι./Όχι.   ne/o·hi

Please.
Παρακαλώ.   pa·ra·ka·lo

Thank you.
Ευχαριστώ.   ef·ha·ri·sto

Sorry.
Συγγνώμη.   sigh·no·mi

What's your name?
Πώς σας λένε;   pos sas le·ne

My name is ...
Με λένε ...   me le·ne ...

Do you speak English?
Μιλάτε αγγλικά;   mi·la·te an·gli·ka

I (don't) understand.
(Δεν)   (dhen)
καταλαβαίνω.   ka·ta·la·ve·no

Eating & Drinking

I'd like ...   Θα ήθελα ...   tha i·the·la...

a cup of coffee   ένα φλυτζάνι καφέ   e·na fli·dza·ni ka·fe

a table   ένα τραπέζι   e·na tra·pe·zi

for two   για δύο α άτομ   ya dhi·o a·to·ma

one beer   μία μπύρα   mi·a bi·ra

I'm a vegetarian.
Είμαι χορτοφάγος.
i·me hor·to·fa·ghos

What would you recommend?
Τι θα συνιστούσες;
ti tha si·ni·stu·ses

Cheers!
Εις υγείαν!
is i·yi·an

That was delicious.
Ήταν νοστιμότατο.
i·tan no·sti·mo·ta·to

Please bring the bill.
Το λογαριασμό, παρακαλώ.
to lo·ghar·ya·zmo pa·ra·ka·lo

Shopping

I'd like to buy ...
Θέλω ν' αγοράσω ...
the·lo na·gho·ra·so ...

I'm just looking.
Απλώς κοιτάζω.
ap·los ki·ta·zo

How much is it?
Πόσο κάνει;
po·so ka·ni

It's too expensive.
Είναι πολύ ακριβό.
i·ne po·li a·kri·vo

Can you lower the price?
Μπορείς να   bo·ris na
κατεβάσεις   ka·te·va·sis
την τιμή;   tin ti·mi

Emergencies

Help!
Βοήθεια!
vo·i·thya

Call a doctor!
Φωνάξτε ένα γιατρό!
fo·nak·ste e·na yi·a·tro

Call the police!
Φωνάξτε την αστυνομία!
fo·nak·ste tin a·sti·no·mi·a

There's been an accident.
Έγινε ατύχημα.
ey·i·ne a·ti·hi·ma

I'm ill.   Είμαι άρρωστος.
                 i·me a·ro·stos

It hurts here. Πονάει εδώ.
                 po·na·i e·dho

I'm lost   Έχω χαθεί.
                 e·kho kha·thi

Time & Numbers

What time is it?
Τι ώρα είναι; ti o·ra i·ne

It's (two o'clock).
Είναι (δύο η ώρα).
i·ne (dhi·o i o·ra)

yesterday χθες   hthes

today σήμερα   si·me·ra

tomorrow αύριο   av·ri·o

morning πρωί   pro·i

afternoon απόγευμα
                 a·po·yev·ma

evening βράδυ   vra·dhi

1	ένας/μία	e·nas/mi·a (m/f)
	ένα	e·na (n)
2	δύο	dhi·o
3	τρεις	tris (m&f)
	τρία	tri·a (n)
4	τέσσερεις	te·se·ris (m&f)
	τέσσερα	te·se·ra (n)
5	πέντε	pen·de
6	έξη	e·xi
7	επτά	ep·ta
8	οχτώ	oh·to
9	εννέα	e·ne·a
10	δέκα	dhe·ka

Transport & Directions

Where is ...?
Πού είναι ...;
pu i·ne ...

What's the address?
Ποια είναι η
pia i·ne i
διεύθυνση;
dhi·ef·thin·si

Can you show me (on the map)?
Μπορείς να μου
bo·ris na mu
δείξεις (στο χάρτη);
dhik·sis (sto khar·ti)

I want to go to ...
Θέλω να πάω στο/στη ...
the·lo na pao sto/sti ...

Where do I buy a ticket?
Πού αγοράζω εισιτήριο;
pu a·gho·ra·zo i·si·ti·ri·o

What time does it leave?
Τι ώρα φεύγει;
ti o·ra fev·yi

Does it stop at ...?
Σταματάει στο ...;
sta·ma·ta·i sto ...

I'd like to get off at ...
Θα ήθελα να κατεβώ ...
tha i·the·la nana ka·te·vo ...

Behind the Scenes

Send Us Your Feedback

We love to hear from travellers – your comments help make our books better. We read every word, and we guarantee that your feedback goes straight to the authors. Visit **lonelyplanet.com/contact** to submit your updates and suggestions.

Note: We may edit, reproduce and incorporate your comments in Lonely Planet products such as guidebooks, websites and digital products, so let us know if you don't want your comments reproduced or your name acknowledged. For a copy of our privacy policy visit lonelyplanet.com/privacy.

Acknowledgements

Front cover photograph: Theatre of Dionysus, Christopher Chan/Getty ©
Back cover photograph: Fishing Net on Boat, Pancrazio Spinelli/EyeEm/Getty ©
Photographs pp29-30 (from left): Songquan Deng; Martidis Ioannis; saiko3p/Shutterstock ©; Adrienne Pitts/Lonely Planet ©

Zora's Thanks

Ευχαριστώ to Vasilis Kakridonis and Lenia Economou, who kindly shared the secrets of their favourite neighbourhoods; to Abdul Ali Rahimi, who was up for everything; to Peter Moskos, whose vision of Athens always informs mine; and to all the Greek singers whose voices carried me through the writing. Also thanks to Brana Vladisavljevic for being an understanding editor, and to Alexis Averbuck for all the work on previous editions.

This Book

This 5th edition of Lonely Planet's *Pocket Athens* guidebook was researched and written by Zora O'Neill. This guidebook was produced by the following:

Destination Editor
Brana Vladisavljevic

Senior Product Editors
Sandie Kestell,
Elizabeth Jones

Product Editor
Alison Killilea

Cartographers
Julie Sheridan,
Anthony Phelan

Book Designer
Gwen Cotter

Assisting Editors
Judith Bamber, Joel Cotterell, Bruce Evans, Gabrielle Stefanos

Cover Researcher
Hannah Blackie

Thanks to Ronan Abayawickrema, Maria Casadei, Kostas Dalaklidis, Ana Granados, Clare Healy, Sonia Kapoor, Sheila Kunwar, Amy Lynch, Martine Power, Simon Richmond, Ross Taylor, Robert Williams Kvalvaag, Helle Work

Index

See also separate subindexes for:
- Eating p189
- Drinking p190
- Entertainment p190
- Shopping p191

Sights 000
Map Pages **000**

Our Writer

Zora O'Neill

Zora visited Greece for the first time in 1995, and has been getting her summer sardine fix there ever since. A writer for Lonely Planet since 2005, she is also the author of *All Strangers Are Kin*, a travel memoir about studying Arabic in the Middle East. She lives in Queens, New York, in (not entirely coincidentally) a Greek neighbourhood where frappés, feta and fresh herbs are plentiful.

Published by Lonely Planet Global Limited
CRN 554153
5th edition – Mar 2022
ISBN 978 1 78868 047 9
© Lonely Planet 2022 Photographs © as indicated 2022
10 9 8 7 6 5 4 3 2 1
Printed in Singapore

Although the authors and Lonely Planet have taken all reasonable care in preparing this book, we make no warranty about the accuracy or completeness of its content and, to the maximum extent permitted, disclaim all liability arising from its use.